Help! Let Me Out of Here!

Kathryn Lamb lives 'quietly' in Gillingham, Dorset, with her husband, Adrian Bovey, and their six children and two hamsters. Adrian has three teenage children.

Without the help of all these people (not so much the hamsters) she would have found it a lot more difficult to write this book. She would like to thank them all, including some very special grandparents.

Kathryn draws cartoons for *Private Eye* and *The Oldie*. She has illustrated a number of books for Piccadilly Press including: FOR WEDDINGS, A FUNERAL AND WHEN YOU CAN'T FLUSH THE LOO; YOU'RE MY BEST FRIEND – I HATE YOU; A RIGHT ROYAL HISTORY; THE GOOD, THE BAD AND THE GHASTLY: WORLD WAR II and THE GOOD, THE BAD AND THE GHASTLY: THE WILD WEST.

This is the third book in the *Help!* series, and the first two books were extremely well-reviewed. HELP! MY FAMILY IS DRIVING ME CRAZY! was selected by *The Bookseller* as one of a hundred best books for Spring 1997: '. . . *it hits just the right humorous note.*'

Other titles in this seris:
HELP! MY FAMILY IS DRIVING ME CRAZY!
HELP! MY SOCIAL LIFE IS A MESS!

Help! Let Me Out of Here!

YOUR GUIDE TO TAKING THE STRESS OUT OF SCHOOL

●

Kathryn Lamb

Piccadilly Press • London

for Frances and everyone at Beaminster School, Dorset

Designed by Paul Cooper

Phototypeset by Piccadilly Press
Printed and bound by WBC, Bridgend
for the publishers Piccadilly Press Ltd,
5 Castle Road, London NW1 8PR

A catalogue record for this book is available from the British Library

ISBNs: 1 85340 575 2 (hardback)
1 85340 570 1 (trade paperback)

Contents

Introduction

RRRIIIIIINNGG!!!
(The bell from hell)

There is an expression: "saved by the bell". This is certainly true when a particularly difficult or boring lesson is brought to a sudden end by the sound of the bell going off. You are only too happy to join in the mass stampede for the nearest door.

The sound of bells is a noise with which you are likely to become very familiar over the next few years. The adults

FOR WHOM THE BELL TOLLS
(IT TOLLS FOR YOU WHEN YOU HAVE FORGOTTEN TO DO YOUR MATHS HOMEWORK)

in your life will, from time to time, bend your ear with a little lecture on the dangers of listening to loud music, especially at discos. "It is very bad for your ears. You will go deaf. What? What did you say? Speak up, for goodness sake, I can't hear you when you mumble like that!" In the next breath they will ask you if you have set your alarm for the morning: "You've got to get up for school, you know!" They have thoughtfully bought you an innocent-looking little alarm-clock with a bell so loud it detonates your eardrums at seven every morning. After this, your entire day will be punctuated, at regular intervals, by the loud and insistent ringing of the bell, signalling the beginning or the end of lessons. There is another expression: "for whom the bell tolls", referring to your imminent doom, when summoned to a maths lesson for which you are totally unprepared (you can think of 1,649 places you would rather be and 2,935 things you would rather be doing).

Schooldays – the happiest days of your life. This may be a slight exaggeration (or even totally untrue) for most people. The person who made this remark was probably looking back at their schooldays through rose-coloured spectacles. In other words, they were just recalling the good times, and forgetting all the days when they fell out with their friends or forgot to do their homework. Some people really do enjoy school, and their enthusiasm is either infectious or irritating, depending on your attitude.

The truth is you will most certainly have some happy and memorable days at school, but you should also be prepared for days when everything does not go quite so smoothly. But don't get stressed. Get yourself de-stressed, instead.

Who's that boy?/Who's that girl?

Here are the main characters you will meet:

● Angelica Toogood

Angelica is nearly fifteen, and is the elder daughter of Mr and Mrs Toogood.

Mr Toogood is a bank manager, and Mrs Toogood is a housewife/homemaker and an expert cake-baker.

Angelica has an older brother, Grant, who is mega brainy and reads a lot of books. Her younger sister, Becky, is eleven, and she likes to try out Angelica's make-up and borrow her clothes.

● Basil Broke - Baz

Baz is fourteen and an only child, whose parents are divorced. He lives with his mother, Mrs Broke.

Every other weekend he stays with his father, Mr Broke, and his father's new wife, Celia. Celia has four children of her own: Leonora, Theodora, Henrietta and William. Baz's father and Celia have recently had a baby called Henry. The children make loads of noise, and Baz finds it hard to get enough sleep. Baz blames his father for the fact that his mother is always broke, and has to go out to work (in a fish shop). However, his father pays for Baz's saxophone lessons.

KEY TO FAMILY TREE :

A GRANDMA B COLIN THE HAMSTER C BECKY

D STANLEY THE CAT E MR TOOGOOD F GRANDPA

G GRANT TOOGOOD H MRS TOOGOOD I HORACE

J ANGELICA

Introduction

KEY TO FAMILY TREE :

A BASIL BROKE ('BAZ') (HE'S INTO JAZZ)

B 'FISH'

C MRS BROKE

KEY TO FAMILY TREE :
A MR BROKE, MRS CELIA BROKE and HOWLIN' HENRY THE HALF-BROTHER B BASIL BROKE ('BAZ') C LEONORA, THEODORA AND HENRIETTA D WILLIAM E MR and MRS RABBIT

Soumik Sen

Soumik is thirteen. He is an only child with two doting parents, and many relations. There are frequent family gatherings, which Soumik does not enjoy, since his girl cousins (there are seventeen of them) tend to whisper together and giggle a lot. As the only boy, he is the focus of everyone's attention.

KEY TO FAMILY TREE :

A SOUMIK SEN
B MR AND MRS SEN
C AUNT ANEENA AND HER 2 DAUGHTERS
D AUNT SITA AND HER 5 DAUGHTERS
E AUNT PRITI AND HER 4 DAUGHTERS
F AUNT JASMEENA AND HER 6 DAUGHTERS

KEY TO FAMILY TREE :
A STEVE CASH B JAMES CASH
C MR CASH D MRS CASH

Steve Cash

Steve is fifteen. His parents run their own businesses, and they are too busy most of the time to take much notice of Steve, or his younger brother, James (thirteen).

Steve has formed his own band, and he frequently upsets the neighbours by making too much noise. He thinks he is pretty cool, but he sometimes feels lonely, and Baz is his only real friend.

Amy Average

Amy is fourteen. Her little brother, Anthony, is eight. Mr Average is currently out of work, so the family derives its income from Mrs Average's job as a music teacher.

Angelica and Amy are best friends (except when they fall out).

KEY TO FAMILY TREE :

A AMY B ANTHONY ('PEST') C GRAN

D MR AVERAGE E MRS AVERAGE

F 'SQUAWK' THE PARROT

QUIZ

How school-wise are you? Or, how is your classroom/ corridor/canteen cred? Answer these questions and find out how much of a cool school dude you really are.

1) What do you do in your lunch-break?

a) You eat your lunch. It consists of a wholemeal, vegetarian, salad sandwich, a wholegrain snack bar and an apple, occasionally with a dried prune or two thrown in as a treat. You chew every mouthful carefully for at least three minutes, and usually retire to the lavatory afterwards, taking a school textbook with you to study.

b) You join your friends in the canteen for banana sandwiches/vegetable risotto/lasagne and chips or whatever (usually whatever), and then take part in one of the lunch-time clubs, such as music, netball, swimming or trampolining (particularly good immediately after lasagne and chips).

c) Nothing very much. You have some chips, stuff yourself with sweets, read a magazine and get sent to see the year head for eating in the classroom/corridor, leaving your bag where people can trip over it, and wearing an untidy purple shirt.

2) What do you do in lessons?

a) Concentrate. Hard.

b) You listen to what other people are saying. This quite often includes the teacher. You make a sincere effort to stay awake.

MAKING A SINCERE EFFORT
TO STAY AWAKE GOES DOWN
WELL WITH MOST TEACHERS

c) You chew gum whenever the teacher isn't looking at you. Or, if it is a teacher you don't like (silly statement, since you don't like any teachers), you chew gum on purpose when they are looking at you. You try to catch up on lost sleep, and become exceedingly ill-tempered when the teacher taps you smartly on the shoulder and wakes you up to ask you what the capital of Albania is.

3) How do you get through a crowded corridor?
a) You say "excuse me". When everyone ignores you, you say it again, a little more loudly, but always politely. When you find your way still blocked, a sense of despair and panic sets in, because you do not wish to be late for double geography.

"Excuse me!" you exclaim. "Would it not be sensible if everyone were to walk in single file? Everyone going to geography should keep to the right, while those who have no business in this part of the school at this time of day should leave on the left." Shortly after this speech you are rendered senseless by someone swinging a schoolbag round and round at head height.

b) You push and shove like the rest of them (and with the best of them), but not roughly.

c) You swing a schoolbag round and round at head height, and knock people flying in all directions, shouting rudely at them to get out of your way.

4) You find a year seven pupil hopelessly lost in the corridor. What is your reaction?

a) You put a comforting arm round their shoulders, explain that it is a very caring school and that they mustn't worry or get upset. Then you realise you are late for metalwork and rush away, leaving them still standing in the corridor, none the wiser.

b) You march them off to where they want to go. Before leaving them, you get out your biro and draw a condensed map of the school on the palm of their hand (and continuing up the arm as far as the elbow).

c) You mutter darkly at them, "Look, kid, this school's a dump. We're all lost before we even get here. Know what I mean?" Then you give them a friendly shove on the back and leave them lying face down in the corridor.

5) How do you wear your tie?

a) Carefully knotted and very straight and neat.

b) Loosely knotted with a short, fat bit at the front and a long, thin bit hanging down behind. The end of it is frayed where you have chewed it, and many of the threads are missing where you have carefully pulled them out during a boring lesson. Alternatively, you may favour the micro tie style (see illustration).

STYLES OF TIE CONT.

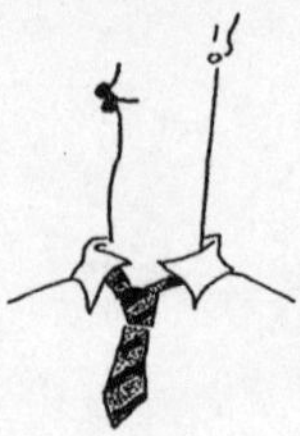

MICRO TIE (CLOSE UP)
IN EXTREME CASES MICRO TIE IS SCARCELY VISIBLE TO THE NAKED EYE

DIFFERENT STYLES OF SCHOOL TIE

DIFFERENT STYLES OF SCHOOL TIE

c) On the days when you remember to wear it, it usually ends up tied round your head, bandanna-style, or attached to your schoolbag and used to drag the bag along the floor.

6) How do you wear your shirt?
a) If the shirt is white, it will be a dazzling, almost unearthly white, with all the buttons, including the collar, done up, and carefully tucked in all round (and in extreme cases, tucked into your underpants).

IN EXTREME CASES THE SHIRT IS TUCKED INTO THE UNDERPANTS (BUT IT ALWAYS ESCAPES IN THE END)

b) If the shirt was white, it isn't any longer (since your father put it in a non-fast coloured wash). You tuck part of it in, and another part comes untucked. You prefer it untucked with the top button, or two buttons, undone. The cuffs are frayed where you have chewed them during a boring or stressful lesson.

c) You have dyed your shirt purple on purpose, not because you particularly like purple, but because you know the school particularly doesn't. You prefer a shirt at least four sizes too large, worn loose and flowing (or flapping) to the knees, with all the buttons undone (if you are a boy).

● **If you chose mostly As:** You will probably do well at school, but you will be considered by many to be a goody-goody and a teacher's pet. This may make you a little isolated, especially if you spend all your time with your nose in a schoolbook or locked in the lavatory (steady up on those prunes or your "little problem" could escalate into a worse problem). Mark Bookmark is an example of this type. His classmates find him strange and stand-offish because he seems to prefer the company of books to them, and they may call him names like "swot" (or worse). It is worth considering that Mark may be intensely shy and he is quite possibly hiding behind his books because he feels safer there. (He may also quite simply enjoy his work, and there is nothing wrong with this as long as you strike the right balance between work and relaxation. See Chapter Three: Work: Problem Four.) This does not apply to the incredibly beautiful or funny people, such as Arabella Proudfoot or Jeremy Jollysport, who manage to get away with being teacher's pets while also maintaining their popularity with their peers (how do they do it?). Arabella dances beautifully and, generally speaking, never puts a foot wrong, although it is just as well to bear in mind that she is only human and could trip up at any time.

● **If you chose mostly Bs:** You have got it about right. You strike the right balance between being part of the school crowd, all laughing, talking, pushing and pulling together. But, for the most part, not in such a way as to upset the teaching staff and cause problems for everyone, including yourself. Examples of type B at St Herbert's school are Amy Average, Soumik Sen, Baz Broke and Angelica Toogood. Occasionally Angelica sinks into category C and has to be rescued by her friends.

● **If you chose mostly Cs:** Oh dear! You have an attitude problem. Your attitude towards school is negative, confrontational and antagonistic. You will probably have to look these words up in a dictionary because you have slept through every English lesson so far. You tend to stay up late every night, and are therefore too tired to cope with school. Living on a diet of Coke, chips and sweets also tends to make you feel ill and, if you are prone to spots, will certainly make them worse. You tend to upset people by being provocative the whole time and, since you are likely to get your friends into trouble as well as yourself, you will almost certainly alienate-a-mate. But it is never too late to change. Steve Cash is aware of his faults and is conscious of the fact that his younger brother, James, tends to copy his bad attitude. From time to time Steve makes a genuine effort to turn over a new leaf, with varying degrees of success.

●CHAPTER 1 A New Day! Rise And Shine!

PROBLEM 1: Waking up

Waking up can be a shock to the system at the best of times, but especially when you are suddenly jolted out of a delicious dream about the love of your life into . . . a typical Monday morning. Just how much of a shock it is depends on a number of things:

1) How prepared you are for the day ahead.
2) What time you wake up.
3) What time you went to bed the night before.
4) What kind of parent you have.

There are four main categories of parent:

a) The parent who strokes your hair gently and whispers: "It's time to get up, dear. I've brought your cup of tea." It must be emphasised that this kind of parent is VERY RARE. If you have a parent like this, you are incredibly lucky. Don't tell anyone where you live, or you will be besieged by people wanting to move in with you and adopt your parent as their own.

b) The parent who hammers on your door and shouts, "GET UP! YOU'RE GOING TO BE LATE!" This is a more normal variety of parent. This is the parent who was not at all keen on the idea of getting out of bed themselves, has just caught sight of themselves and the bags under their eyes in the mirror, and is therefore likely to take out their early-morning ill humour on you. Don't shout back at them. You will only make matters worse. They will probably feel better after several cups of coffee.

c) The enthusiastic parent. This kind of parent expects you to be up early, fresh-faced and full of zest for the day ahead. They remember their schooldays as one long party and can't understand why your face is so long that your chin keeps hitting the floor. They insist you eat a hearty breakfast to "set you up for the day", and they expect you to walk to school, as the fresh air (and driving rain) will help clear your head, so that it is ready to receive exciting new facts and figures (as long as you don't die of pneumonia first).

You definitely need to get yourself organised, if you have a parent who is noticeable by their absence (or perhaps they are simply still asleep with no intention of getting up yet. This is just adding insult to injury, as far as you are concerned – they might at least get up to bid you a fond farewell).

The scene

Steve Cash's parents start work early, and are usually gone from the house or, at least, busy on the phone arranging business deals by the time Steve surfaces. They don't bother waking him up, and Steve has occasionally half woken up, gone back to sleep and missed school altogether. He found himself in a certain amount of trouble as a result, and a letter was sent to his parents, who threatened to withdraw his allowance if he failed to get himself to school on time.

What should you do if you persistently oversleep?

● **Boring but obvious things to do:** Buy an alarm-clock. If you sleep through the alarm, get a louder one. If you still sleep through it, buy six alarm-clocks and time them to go off consecutively or all at once, depending on how strong your nerves are. You can get some amusing alarms, such as a cockerel crowing, or a cartoon character shouting, "Time to get up! Walkies!" at his dog, among others. How amused you will be at seven a.m. on a damp and dismal Monday morning in late January, time alone will tell.

You will definitely not be amused at all when one of your alarms, a teasmade (a kind of alarm-clock which wakes you up with a nice cup of tea), kindly donated by an aunt, goes berserk and wakes you up at three a.m. with a nice cup of tea.

● **Inspired (possibly) thing to do:** Get a friend to phone you when they wake up. Of course, this solution falls flat on its face if your friend also oversleeps. In which case, you could ask Beverley McBrisk, also in your class and an energetic, sporty type, given to early-morning aerobics, to give you a wake-up call. This may not go down well with your father when, bleary-eyed, he puts the receiver to his ear and is nearly knocked sideways by an enthusiastic blast from McBrisk: "Come on! Come on! Get those arms and legs moving! Wakey-wakey! Move it! Reach for the sky! See ya! Byeee!" Beverley McBrisk may also risk incurring the wrath of her parents by running up their phone bill in making repeated wake-up calls.

● **A gentler way to wake up:** The radio alarm-clock. You will wake to the soothing sound of music (unless it's Dr Drear and the Deadheads, which it is very likely to be if you have tuned in to the new funk/techno/rock station). You may have to leave the volume turned up high in order to wake you up.

Please note: the use of earplugs at night is inadvisable, since none of the above solutions will work if you do. Similarly, sleeping with a pillow/duvet over your head is not a good idea, and it also tends to cut off your oxygen supply. You need a good supply of oxygen to the brain in order to cope with schoolwork, especially maths.

● **The ideal (oh yeah?) solution:** All you really need is a manic dog or cat who will leap on you first thing in the morning. This will wake you up. A dog is likely to drool and generally slobber over your face, while a cat will launch a sudden (and savage), surprise attack on your toes (there are few things more irritating to a cat than the sight of human toes, especially when they wiggle). You may not be totally thrilled to be woken up in this way by the faithful hound or the playful pussy cat if you have already been kept awake half the night by the incredible and insistent noise of your younger sibling's hamster trundling away for hours on its little wheel. Talking of which, you can certainly rely on THEM to wake you up in the morning. No, I don't mean hamsters, although you could try training them to do so. I am, of course, referring to your younger siblings, who do a brilliant job of disturbing the entire household first thing in the morning, regardless of whether it is a schoolday or the weekend.

If there is just one younger sibling, he/she will wake you up because he/she is bored or wants

RISE AND SHINE!

something. If there are two or more of them, they will have a fierce argument right outside your bedroom door, and one of them will probably start howling.

So now you are awake.

PROBLEM 2: Getting dressed (school uniform/school clothes)

● The scene - 1

Baz is unable to find a clean, matching pair of socks. The only matching pair he can find are the ones he has been wearing for the last week, and they are now standing up by themselves in a corner of the room (and very soon they will be walking out by themselves, if they don't make it to the next wash). Baz opens the door of the airing cupboard. This is a bad mistake, since everything falls out on top of him. But there are no socks – apart from a few more odd ones. What should he do?

● Bad solution: Skip school altogether. You are unlikely to get a sympathetic reaction when you explain that your absence was due to lack of socks.

● Better solution: Wear odd socks. Baz has always had a natural preference for odd socks, usually in varying shades of luminous green, orange and purple. It is probably tactful to choose a more subdued shade for school. You can feel reasonably certain that the teachers at your school have better things to do than conduct a rigorous inspection of a thousand or more pairs of socks. This applies, to a greater or lesser extent, to the rest of your school uniform. As long as you wear the correct school colours (sludge green, dried-prune black, murky maroon, navy blue), you can interpret your school uniform to suit your own personality. Most schools are fairly flexible about this, although you should beware of bending the rules too far.

The scene - 2

Angelica decides to wear her ankle-length, black skirt to St

DIAGRAM TO ILLUSTRATE REASONS FOR NOT WEARING VERY LONG SKIRT TO SCHOOL

DIAGRAM TO ILLUSTRATE REASON FOR NOT WEARING VERY SHORT SKIRT TO SCHOOL

Herbert's, hoping that no one will mind (the rules stipulate that skirts should be no more than mid-calf in length). Unfortunately, it's a wet day and she steps in a deep puddle getting off the school bus (school-bus drivers always park carefully so that the door is right over a puddle – more of this later). The bottom of her skirt gets wet and muddy and flaps uncomfortably round her ankles for the rest of the morning. To make matters worse, in the mad rush for the canteen she trips over her skirt and falls down several stairs.

The moral of this: Occasionally there are sound reasons behind seemingly meaningless rules.

The scene - 3

Baz hates his school tie. He hates any tie. Wearing one gives him a headache. His tutor is unsympathetic and quotes the school rule at him: "Ties must be worn at all times, they may be removed in very hot weather and then only with the headteacher's permission."

Baz decides to get his own back. The following day he comes to school wearing only his tie, and no shirt. When his tutor reprimands him, he says, "But, sir, the rules only say that ties must be worn at all times. They don't say that you have to wear a shirt all the time."

CLASS WIT (OR CLASS TWIT?)

● **Likely reaction of the teacher to someone doing stupid things with their uniform:** Narrowing of the eyes, pursing of the lips, smoke coming out of ears, tendency to say things like, "Report immediately to your year head/copy out the school rules six hundred times today after school." This is especially likely to be the case if a joke like Baz's tie-without-shirt gag catches on, and you are the eleventh person so far this morning to be found wearing only a tie and giving the same answer (obviously this joke would be reserved for the boys, unless you really want to get yourself excluded).

Taking the stress out of school uniform/school clothes:

1) Make sure you have your clothes and sports kit organised the night before. Soumik likes to arrange his clothes in a straight line across his bedroom floor so that he steps out of bed straight into his socks (more or less), then steps into his underpants, trousers and shirt, and so on until he reaches his shoes, which are right by the bedroom door. Obviously this is taking things to extremes, but if you arrange your clothes on a chair nearby, it is less stressful than having to rummage through the drawers, search under the bed, or shout at your sister and accuse her of having taken your skirt, only to find it squashed in the bottom of your schoolbag, since you came home in your cycling shorts yesterday.

2) It may be great fun at school sliding down the banisters, so that you end up with holes in your sweatshirt. It may be irresistible to chew your tie (what else is it there for?) or your cuffs, or pull the threads out of your tie. But why not look after your school clothes and spare your parents the expense involved in replacing damaged items? Then they can put the money you have saved them towards the clothes you really want (really, really want). If you are a complete mess, it is probably not good for your own image, let alone the school's image. If you wear dreary and crumpled clothes, you will feel dreary and crumpled. There is a lot you can do to make school uniform bearable

LOOK AFTER YOUR UNIFORM. YOU CAN HAND IT DOWN TO YOUNGER SIBLINGS (AND THEY WILL DESTROY IT)

and wearable. Girls have more choice than boys, since they can wear either trousers or skirts, tights or socks. Boys have a choice between trousers and trousers, and socks and socks. The school will probably insist on crease-resistant shirts, but they have not bargained on your washing machine's ability to crease anything, and your parent's dubious ability to iron even more creases into an already crumpled garment.

PROBLEM 3: Getting ready, getting steady, getting go(ing)

● The scene

Amy Average oversleeps as usual, and is woken by Mrs Average shouting round the door, "You've got ten minutes to get to the bus, Amy!" Amy's first thought is, Have I got time to put my make-up on? Her second thought is, Where's my make-up bag? She has a frantic search and discovers the make-up bag in the side pocket of her schoolbag. She manages to get her make-up on, get dressed and brush her teeth in the space of five minutes. She grabs her schoolbag and makes a mad dash for the school bus. It takes her most of the journey to catch her breath and remember all the things she has forgotten. This is known as being DISORGANISED. It is a condition affecting a large proportion of the human race, and you are by no means the only person who ever forgot to brush your hair/teeth, pack your books and homework into your bag, kiss the dog before you leave. There are certain simple measures you can take to limit the damage caused by being disorganised:

1) Make a list of the things you have to remember. It sometimes helps to write things down. Try not to lose the list.

2) Employ one of the tactics mentioned in Problem One to enable you to get up in good time. This will give you time to sort out your thoughts. Your first thought should not be, Do I have time to put on my make-up? (leaving aside the fact that you are not supposed to wear make-up in school, anyway), but more along the lines of, Ah! I'm awake! Time for a yawn, a big stretch, a few gentle toe-flexing exercises . . . In other words, ease yourself into the day gently, make yourself a cup of tea or coffee, and take it from there. While you steam open your pores over a hot cup of tea, you can consider what you need to take with you today. You have time to check that you have everything you need (lucky you). You have time to freshen up. You could even take a shower, or wash your hair. There is a very good deodorant called Sport, for people who like to charge around the school playing fields. They have not yet marketed one called School, for people who break out in a cold sweat at the very thought of five hours of lessons.

Note to people who are allergic to mornings: If you really can't wake up in good time and you know you're terrible in the mornings, make sure everything is packed and ready the night before. When the alarm goes, all you

MAKE SURE YOU ARE FULLY PREPARED FOR THE DAY AHEAD

need to do is switch into auto school mode (into uniform, on to bus, etc.). Since you don't have to think about anything, having thought about everything the night before, you can wake up gently in your own time (probably halfway through double biology).

3) Breakfast is said to be an important meal, and you should make time to sit down and enjoy it. Not everyone is a breakfast enthusiast. At one end of the spectrum you get Matt Muscleman, a member of the school Rugby team, who regards six Shredded Wheat, fried egg and bacon, followed by several rounds of toast and marmalade, as a light snack. At the other end of the spectrum is Fiona Fillyfeather, who skips breakfast, allows herself a spoonful of cottage cheese and half an apple for lunch and then stuffs herself with four chocolate bars on the school bus coming

THE GREAT BRITISH BREAKFAST

home, if she hasn't already been sent home after passing out during double biology.

Somewhere between these two extremes there is probably you, running to catch the bus with a piece of toast held aloft in one hand, like some kind of Olympic beacon (not Olympic bacon), which you then eat in the bus on the journey to school (but don't drop crumbs down the driver's neck or get butter and marmalade on the seats).

PROBLEM 4: Getting to school

● The scene

Baz lives a kilometre away from St Herbert's Secondary Modern (not nearly far enough, in his opinion). Some days, if he is feeling energetic, he walks there or goes on his skateboard (this caused confusion one day when his gran asked him how he got to school and he replied, "I board". She became very agitated and wanted to know how on earth Mrs Broke was managing to pay boarding fees). On other days, he goes by school bus. The bus is usually fairly full by the time it gets to Baz's stop. How does he manage to get a good seat (near the back)?

● Good solution: He gets Steve (who lives five kilometres away) to reserve a seat for him. It's quite a pleasant way to break yourself into yet another schoolday if you can sit beside your best mate on the journey in.

COOL WAY TO GET TO SCHOOL
(UNTIL YOU FALL OFF)

Slightly dodgy solution: You can bribe a year seven pupil to give up his/her seat for you by promising to reserve a place for him/her at the front of the queue in the canteen. This is all right if you keep your side of the bargain. You can then refer to it every time you want them to give up their seat: "Look, I did keep a place for you at the front of the queue the other day – so you give me your seat."

● **Bad solution:** You take a year seven pupil and pull them off the seat. This is known as bullying. Sitting on them is almost as bad (and very uncomfortable), and both of these actions will certainly incur the wrath of the driver (see below).

Facts about the school bus:

1) It is likely to be old and rickety, inclined to make strange whining, clicking and scrunching noises when travelling uphill (or downhill). It may lean slightly to one side, so that you have to compensate by leaning in the other direction.

2) Anyone who prides themselves on their bus cred will want to sit at the back, safely out of earshot of the driver (this is what you think – beware the driver with bionic ears!). There is usually a pecking order so that the older pupils hog the best seats at the back.

3) There will always be some idiot, or several idiots, who try to upset or embarrass you with loud personal remarks, such as, "Do you shave your legs?" – or they are just generally abusive. IGNORE THEM. If they find that they cannot wind you up, they will lose interest and leave you alone.

4) The nature of your journey to and from school depends largely on the nature of the bus driver, who usually falls into one of several categories (as long as he does not fall asleep, you are all right):

a) THE OVER-CAUTIOUS DRIVER. This one drives at a snail's pace and occasionally stops to let a snail cross the road (or overtake him). You will get to school safely, but probably late.

SLOW BUS DRIVER

b) THE DRIVER WHO MISSED HIS/HER VOCATION AS A FORMULA ONE RACING DRIVER. This one takes corners on two wheels only, screeches to a halt at every stop so that you are thrown forwards, and, if you had breakfast, you may well lose it on the journey. But don't expect any sympathy from the driver if this happens. You will arrive at school early, with a face as white as your shirt used to be, and legs like jelly.

DIFFERENT STYLES OF BUS DRIVER:
THE ONE WHO MISSED HIS VOCATION AS A
FORMULA ONE RACING DRIVER

c) THE JOKER. If you answer back to this one, he is likely to stop the bus, order you off and chase you round it twice, or even three times, to the great delight, cheers and jeers of the assembled audience inside the bus. Unless you are ready for this sort of thing, just laugh at his jokes and otherwise keep quiet.

d) THE BAD-TEMPERED DRIVER. This one hates young people and hates noise. Which is why he is a school bus driver. Keep your head down and don't upset him.

Travelling by bus is not the only way to get to school.

● The scene

Belinda Bossington-Boots's mother drives her in every morning and home again every night in her Range Rover. Angelica wishes that her own mother would drive her to school every day. How can she persuade her to do this?

● The wrong approach: "Mum, why can't you drive me to school like Belinda's mother does? They've got just as far to travel as we have, and Belinda's mum doesn't mind at all." There is a saying that "comparisons are odious", and your parent will not appreciate being compared (unfavourably) with someone else's parent. They are likely to refuse your request.

● A better approach: "Mum, if you'd be really kind and drive me to school today, I'll tidy my room when I get back, and if you collect me later I'll do the washing-up as well." Striking some sort of bargain along these lines may or may not work, depending upon your parent's willingness to co-operate or their situation. They may have to go to work or be too busy to ferry you around.

● **The best you can hope for:** Rain. Even the most hard-hearted of parents may think twice about pushing their offspring out through the door to walk or wait for the bus in a torrential downpour. However, don't be too disappointed if the best they can come up with is, "You can borrow my umbrella, dear. And this plastic rain hat is awfully good. It doesn't look terribly smart but it will help keep your hair dry." They may even grab their keys and get the car out (if they have one, and assuming that the other parent hasn't already taken it). Don't be surprised if the car breaks down on the way (heavy rain has this effect on cars, but at least you will miss some lessons). Don't expect your parent to reach for the keys on a brilliantly sunny morning, no matter how many times you say, "It looks like rain. I really think it's going to rain. I can feel it. The birds are flying upside-down. They always do that before it rains . . ." And so on.

If, as in Baz's case, your parent's only vehicle is a battered second-hand, sickly green Reliant Robin, you may prefer NOT to travel to school by car, although it may be preferable to getting soaked. Prepare for any stupid or derogatory comments people at school may make about your car by coming up with your own jokes about it, or a funny nickname ("Sausage" – because it's an old banger). If you don't get embarrassed or defensive, people will get bored with taking your car to pieces (it falls to pieces naturally, without any help).

The de-stress solutions to getting up and getting to school:

1) Get plenty of rest. This does not mean falling asleep during lessons. Try to get to bed earlier so that you can get up earlier and hopefully have more energy to cope with the day ahead. You might even enjoy it, since being fresh and wide-awake puts you in a much better mood generally.

2) Wear a little of your favourite perfume, aftershave or body spray, as the familiar and pleasing perfume will help to relax you (aromatherapy) and remind you of good times and scented days or evenings. Don't use too much or the effect in a crowded classroom with twenty or more different perfumes mingling will be quite overwhelming,

DE-STRESS IDEA : AROMATHERAPY

and Fiona Fillyfeather will probably pass out. Also, someone is bound to say, "What IS that stink?" (Embarrassing, if it turns out to be the biology teacher, Miss Peabody's favourite and very expensive scent, given to her by her boyfriend as an engagement present.)

3) Take time out to enjoy a relaxed breakfast before you leave for school. Bolting your breakfast will add to feelings of stress, as you will probably suffer acute indigestion and hiccup through history or belch through biology for the rest of the morning. Everyone will turn to look at you and laugh at your hiccups, and you may even irritate-a-mate with your persistent burping.

Question: is burping REALLY that funny? Can you explain why? Answers on a postcard, please . . .

4) Get your school uniform/school clothes ready at the beginning of the week. Make certain everything is washed and ironed and then you won't have to raise the I-haven't-got-anything-clean-to-wear alarm. Also, you then don't even have to think about it. Not thinking is a great de-stress solution.

CHAPTER 2 Getting On With It

PROBLEM 1: Getting on with people

QUIZ

Are you a cool school dude or a school fool? Answer these questions and find out.

1) An unfriendly type in one of the upper years says to you challengingly, "What are you staring at?" Everyone listens to hear your reply. Is it:
a) "Nothing. I'm not wearing my contact lenses. I can't see a thing."
b) "I'm staring at your ugly face."
c) "What wonderful hair you have."

2) You're sitting next to one of your mates. You keep fooling around and giving them friendly pushes. You give one friendly push too many, and they end up on the floor with a tremendous crash as their chair tips over. What do you say to the teacher?
a) "I've lost one of my gold studs, Mrs Marchforth. Baz is helping me to find it."
b) "Baz is being a real pain, Mrs Marchforth. He won't leave me alone."
c) "I'm really sorry. It was all my fault. It won't happen again. Are you all right, Baz? Oh, God, I'm so sorry!"

3) In the mad rush for the school canteen, one of the younger pupils trips and falls over. What do you do?
a) You stop and help them up.
b) You trample over them.
c) You help them up and take them straight to the sick bay to make sure they're all right. You express great concern, asking them over and over again if they're OK. By the time you get to the canteen, morning break is over.

4) You notice someone new to your year standing alone and looking forlorn. What do you say to them?
a) "I'm just off to the canteen. Come and meet the gang!"
b) "What are you staring at?"
c) "What wonderful hair you have! And your eyes – they're an incredible shade of blue! Do straight noses run in your family?" (The answer may well be "only when they have a cold".)

5) You have a friend who blushes easily and is very self-conscious about it. You notice that there is a large split in their trousers, of which they seem unaware. What do you do?

a) Take them to one side and tell them very quietly what's happened. Help them to find something else to wear, or help them cover up the split with a jumper or sweatshirt.

b) Take them by the shoulders and turn them round so everyone can see, while shouting at the top of your voice: "LOOK WHO'S FLASHING! HEY – LOOK AT SCOTT, EVERYONE! HE'S GONE THE SAME COLOUR AS HIS UNDERWEAR!" (worrying, if they happen to be tartan).

c) Say to them in your normal voice, audible to quite a number of people, "Oh, god, you're not going to like this! Something really embarrassing's happened! I don't know how to tell you . . ." Giggle, giggle. And then, in a stage whisper, "You've split your trousers!" After all this, you go overboard trying to be helpful, even finding a needle and thread and offering to sew up the split in front of the whole class.

● **If you chose mostly As:** You are a cool school dude. You have an answer for everything (usually), but you are sufficiently charming that you get away with most things without landing yourself or others in trouble. Your friendly manner and kind heart should make people warm to you.

● **If you chose mostly Bs:** Your attitude may alienate-a-mate, unless you can tone it down slightly and show people that you are a cool school dude at heart. Put yourself in other people's shoes (even if you think their bright orange platforms with contrasting laces are decidedly naff – you don't have to say so). Consider how you would feel if someone were to behave towards you in the way you are behaving towards them. Could you handle it? If not, then take time to rethink your attitude. Give yourself (and others) a break.

● **If you chose mostly Cs:** You have many good qualities, which may occasionally be overshadowed by a tendency to go over the top. You can easily overwhelm another person by paying them too many compliments or being in too much of a hurry to help (do they *want* help?). You certainly have a kind heart and a generous nature, but it may be in your best interests to adopt a more laid-back attitude. Try listening to others rather than immediately offering them a whole load of advice to which you may not have given sufficient thought. To avoid being a school fool, chill out and keep your cool. This means less stress.

PROBLEM 2: Getting there (Where?) (Double biology/maths/English) (Where's that?) (It's not in here) (Sorry! I've got the wrong room!) (It's in the science lab) (THAT'S MILES AWAY!) (Sorry I'm late)

The scene

Soumik Sen's tutor group has just finished the morning tutorial period, during which he had a slight falling-out with Steve, whom he was sitting next to, since Steve dropped a handful of woodlice down the back of Soumik's shirt and made him yell. Soumik got into trouble, and Steve didn't, and no one knows what happened to the woodlice. Fortunately, Steve and Soumik are saved by the bell, which means that Steve can escape to the opposite end of the building from Soumik, since they are in different groups for their next lessons. Soumik is tempted to chase Steve down the corridor, down two flights of steps, across a courtyard, through several double doors, along two more corridors and finally up a staircase, but, even if he caught him, he would then have to retrace his footsteps and would be late for drama, and far too out of breath to do justice to his lead part in a rap interpretation of the balcony scene in Romeo and Juliet.

Steve and Soumik meet up again at lunch-time break, by which time Soumik has calmed down – until he finds a woodlouse in his salad. Steve claims it is nothing to do with him and that he does not recognise it as being one of his woodlice, but it is just as well that Steve and Soumik are at opposite ends of the building for their afternoon lessons.

You will find yourself doing a lot of walking in the course of any schoolday. Most of your lessons will be in different parts of the building, sometimes in different blocks, and certainly up and down stairs, down corridors, through various different rooms, and even across wide expanses of grass and playing fields. All your movements have been skilfully choreographed by the person who drew up the timetable (who later collapsed with a nervous breakdown on discovering that the only way to make the timetable work would be to cancel Thursday completely).

Advantages of mobility through the building:

1) Using your legs at regular intervals helps keep you fit.

2) If you have fallen out with the person you were sitting next to in one lesson, the chances are that you will be in a different group for your next lesson and can sit next to someone else.

3) The ten-minute mobility break between lessons gives you a chance to de-stress, chill out, collect your wits (what's left of them) and take a few deep breaths. It is probably a bad idea to try to catch up on your homework during a mobility break, since this will hardly lead to relaxation.

Disadvantages of mobility through the building:

1) Tremendous wear and tear on the fabric of the building due to frequent stampedes along the corridors, up and down the stairs, and so on.

2) Increased chance of finding yourself in the wrong part of the building, at the wrong time.

3) Increased chance of finding yourself in the right place at the right time, only to realise that you have left all the things (often referred to as "stuff") you need in another part of the building.

4) Tremendous confusion and fear of getting lost caused to people new to the school. If your memory and sense of direction are not that good, these feelings can continue to affect you at intervals throughout your school career. (Mr Fogg, the geography teacher at St Herbert's, is always going in the wrong direction and ending up in the wrong place.) But you learn not to worry about it too much. You always get to double French in the end (and then wish you hadn't).

Even those of you with the most appalling sense of direction will be able to find your way, with your eyes closed, to the most important parts of the school building, namely the canteen and the loos (you will be able to find both of these by your sense of smell alone, for good and bad reasons):

1) The canteen: In order to find this, you just join in the general stampede and you will be carried along in the right direction.

● The scene

Soumik is a vegetarian and he enjoys the varied selection of vegetarian meals on offer at St Herbert's. (St Herbert's has achieved the Healthy Schools Award, although this does not mean that you will be arrested and carted away by the health police if you are found eating a plate of chips and nothing else. Allowances will be made for teenage preferences for energy-giving foods such as chips, and the fact that not everyone can afford the smoked salmon salad.)

Soumik does not particularly enjoy the cramped conditions round the table where he has managed to find somewhere to sit. He can hardly move his elbows, which makes eating difficult. To make matters worse, Steve starts a food fight, and launches a sausage into the air – which then lands on Soumik's plate. This is particularly offensive to Soumik, since it is not even a vegetarian sausage. What should Soumik do?

● **Bad thing to do:** Throw the sausage back at Steve. This will get Soumik into trouble as well as Steve, since the school dinner ladies will not be pleased. The school dinner ladies (lunch ladies?) rule (OK). They are wonderful ladies who generally remind you of your own mother, and they don't stand for any nonsense. It is foolish

DIAGRAM TO ILLUSTRATE HOW TO ALIENATE-A-MATE (AND UPSET THE DINNER LADIES)

to risk losing their goodwill, as they can be very sympathetic and helpful when you need someone to talk to.

● **A better thing to do:** Move to another table. Find a sausage-free zone and eat your lunch in peace.

● **A drastic thing to do:** Give up being a vegetarian and eat the sausage.

2) The Loos
Bad things about the loos:

a) The smell. There is not a lot you can do about this,

except bring an enormous can of air freshener. The resulting sickly sweet smell is likely to be as bad in its own way as the smell in the first place.

b) People who unscrew the loo seats and leave them loose. The next time the seat is sat upon (inevitably by you) you are likely to slide off and end up on the floor. The people responsible for this will be heard sniggering just outside. These people are rather sad, as there must be better ways of spending your time than removing loo seats.

c) No loo paper. Or even if there is, it is some kind of parchment which doesn't so much wipe away as wipe

around. You might consider bringing in your own personal supply of loo paper. In the meantime, do ask someone to replace supplies of loo paper and sanitary towels in the dispenser, and so on.

Good things about the loos:

a) You would be in a certain amount of difficulty and discomfort without them.

b) If you are a girl, you can retire to the girls' loo with your friends to refresh your make-up (which you aren't supposed to wear). There are mirrors so you can see yourself. This may or may not be such good news.

c) It is a social gathering place. If the smell is particularly bad, it is more like an anti-social gathering place. It is a good place to hide, but not for too long, or people will think you are ill or have a serious problem.

The de-stress solutions for getting on (and over, and up . . .)

1) Laugh, joke, gossip, feast with your friends, but not during Mr Prenderghastly's maths lessons, or you will be sent straight to the head's office and several black marks will be added to your school report.

2) Remember that school is just one more step along the great path of life. This may or may not be a comforting thought, when you are faced with climbing the enormous flight of steps which leads to the art room for the third time in ten minutes (Mr Potts, the art master, keeps sending you to the Resources Room, conveniently situated on the

other side of the building, for further supplies of materials).

3) Take a deep breath, but probably not if you are anywhere near the loos, or the unpleasant odours may cause you to keel over sideways.

4) Get rid of stress from your system by joining a lunch-time club, such as aerobics, and work out with your friends to music. Any activity involving music and movement, or sport generally (as long as you are not too fiercely competitive) is likely to be relaxing.

5) Find a friend you can confide in. Telling a friend how beastly Miss Peabody was to you, or how horrid that boy in year ten who keeps bumping into you is will help de-stress the situation. It is "good to talk".

CHAPTER 3 Work

The three Rs – Reading, 'Riting and 'Rithmetic

PROBLEM 1: "What's your favourite subject, dear?"

This is a question that doting grandmothers, aunts and various other friends and relations will ask you at intervals throughout your school career. It is just as well to prepare

a suitable answer in advance. You may have to adjust your answers as time goes by . . .

The scene

Amy has always enjoyed drawing, and is keen to impress Mr Potts, the art master, by producing a brilliant work of art. Her group is told to do pencil portraits of each other. Amy decides to do a portrait of Angelica. She has difficulties getting the shape of the face right, and realises that she has made it too square and heavy. In a burst of irritation, she gives it a beard. The eyes are too close together, and Amy puts in some bushy eyebrows to complete the effect, which is not unlike a police photofit picture of a dangerous criminal.

"Is that meant to be me?" says a voice sharply. Amy jumps violently. Mr Potts is looking over her shoulder. Amy is suddenly acutely aware that he has a beard (much smaller and neater than the one on her drawing) and that his eyebrows are quite bushy.

"I am much better looking than that," says Mr Potts. "And I don't have hair growing out of my ears. If you were an accomplished artist, you might get away with an attempt at humour. But I suggest you have a *very* long way to go."

Mr Potts is clearly offended, and Amy realises that she is likely to dig herself a deeper hole if she tries to explain. Her friends are collapsing all around her with barely suppressed mirth, and the more they giggle, the angrier Mr Potts becomes.

Mr Potts and Amy do not see eye to eye (or eyebrow to eyebrow) after this incident.

DIAGRAM TO ILLUSTRATE HOW TO MAKE A BAD SITUATION WORSE

Sad fact: An unfriendly and uninspiring teacher can put you right off a subject which you might have enjoyed, had you received more encouragement. Try not to let them get to you – there'll be other teachers.

● **Happier fact:** For every uninspiring teacher, there are several more who have a real gift for bringing a subject to life, so that you find yourself thinking, almost subconsciously, CHEMISTRY IS FUN.

Teachers can be divided into two main categories:
Teacher-U-Like
Teacher-U-Don't Like

1) Teacher-U-Like: An example is Mrs Macbeth, the English and drama teacher, who turns a blind eye when she notices Angelica applying her lip gloss in the middle of a lesson. As long as Angelica understands why King Lear is not very happy, and knows how to spell "accommodate", she doesn't mind. This kind of teacher is likely to inhale deeply when they are standing beside you and say, "What's that lovely smell?" This can be embarrassing, especially if it's your deodorant they can smell, but at least it's friendly. You can talk easily to this sort of teacher, and they often have a pastoral role. This does not mean that they are a shepherd in their spare time, looking after sheep, but they actually offer advice and counselling, if you have any kind of problem.

A word of warning: Lip gloss is all right, as you can claim you are using it for sore lips. But don't expect your teacher to believe you if you try to argue that you are applying bright crimson Decadent Plum lipstick for the good of your health. It is unwise to push even the most sympathetic teacher's patience too far, since they

TEACHER-U-LIKE

themselves are likely to get into trouble if you break the rules too openly in their lessons.

2) Teacher-U-Don't Like

The scene

Amy has forgotten to do her geography homework. Mr Fogg, the geography teacher, contrasts her unfavourably to Arabella Proudfoot, who always hands in her homework on time. He draws attention, in front of the whole class, to Amy's failure to do her homework, and heaps praise on

Arabella for the wonderful work she has done. After this, he takes every opportunity to pick on Amy for such things as not sitting up straight, looking out of the window, or yawning halfway through his practical demonstration of how slowly a glacier moves. His ability to turn himself into a human glacier is complete when he freezes Amy in mid-yawn with an icy stare. It is clear that Arabella is teacher's pet, whereas Amy is teacher's pet hate. What can Amy do about this?

● **Best thing to do:** Keep quiet, DON'T yawn, but look alert and interested throughout the lesson. Make sure you hand your homework in promptly on the next occasion, and you may find that the teacher begins to thaw (unlike the glacier). If, on the other hand, your teacher shows no signs of melting, this may simply be an NYCD situation (Nothing You Can Do about it). This kind of teacher has favourites and non-favourites, and you are never going to make the transition from non-favourite to favourite unless you suddenly become quite brilliant at their particular subject, and genuinely believe that geography is the BEST. You can avoid making a bad situation worse by NOT sitting at the back of the class and NOT giggling during Mr Fogg's impression of a volcano erupting (he crouches down and then leaps up, flinging his arms wide and shouting, "BOOM!").

Classifying teachers is complicated, and a single species, such as maths teachers, can be sub-divided into many different types:

DO LAUGH AT YOUR TEACHER'S JOKES
DON'T LAUGH WHEN THEY ARE BEING SERIOUS
(IF YOU FIND IT HARD TO TELL THE DIFFERENCE, LOOK AT THE PERSON NEXT TO YOU TO SEE IF THEY ARE LAUGHING. THEN YOU WILL BOTH GET INTO TROUBLE)

1) Embarrassing teacher

The scene

Mr Prenderghastly, the maths master, suddenly, and without warning, breaks off from his explanation of a hundred and one things you can do with an obtuse angle, and says, "Angelica Toogood! What's happened to your hair? You haven't been dyeing it again, have you? If you spent less time dyeing your hair and more time on your maths homework, you might stand more chance of understanding how useful an obtuse angle can be."

Everyone turns to stare at Angelica and her hair, and she feels herself blushing to match the colour of her hair. How should she deal with this?

● **Bad thing to do:** Grin like an idiot and pull silly faces at your classmates. This kind of teacher is trying to make a fool out of you, so don't complete the effect by behaving like one.

● **Even worse thing to do:** Hit back with a clever or rude remark made under your breath, such as, "It's better than having great hairy black caterpillars for eyebrows, like yours." You may have intended that only your friends should hear this remark, but Mr Prenderghastly has bionic ears, and you will be sent to the year head, or even the head, for being rude to a teacher. This sort of behaviour can get you into serious trouble.

● **Best thing to do:** Remain impassive. Show no particular emotion, and the teacher and your classmates will quickly lose interest in you (and your hair). If you are a girl, and conscious of blushing at the slightest provocation, you could try wearing very pale foundation to cover your blushes (don't use too much, or you will be sent straight to the sick bay).

2) Trendy teacher

The scene

Baz has just passed a note to Steve, asking him if he is going to the Jamsplat gig on Friday, at the Blue Porcupine. This happens halfway through double history with Mr Tardis. Mr Tardis intercepts the note and reads it.

"Wow!" exclaims Mr Tardis. "Have you guys really got tickets for Jamsplat? They're a real cool, groovy, happening band, aren't they? I particularly liked their last album, 'Technosandwich'. Did you know that their lead singer, Kevin Jam, was born in Hartlepool, and originally trained as a sous-chef, before breaking out into serious jam?"

Steve is beginning to feel embarrassed, since Mr Tardis knows more about Jamsplat than he does. Baz is fascinated, but doesn't know what to say. He was expecting to get sent to the year head for getting caught, once again, passing notes during a lesson.

Good things about trendy teachers:
They like to feel that they are on a level of mutual understanding and respect with you, because they share your

MR. TARDIS
THE TRENDY ONE

interests, and even try to look like you (Mr Tardis wears fashionable clothes, and is often seen wearing a pair of cool shades, even on a cloudy day). They are prepared to overlook all sorts of minor things, such as passing notes during lessons, that you would normally get into trouble for. Mr Tardis likes to be called Trev.

Bad things about trendy teachers:
The effect of all this can be very disconcerting. Baz doesn't want to call Mr Tardis "Trev". He is not at all sure what to do or say because it is, after all, meant to be a history lesson, and he is aware that certain members of the class cannot stand Jamsplat or their music, and are getting increasingly fed up with Mr Tardis's tendency to get side-tracked. Also, trendy teachers are sometimes unpredictable, and on a bad day they may suddenly snap back into full traditional teacher mode, and you'll find yourself catapulted in the direction of the head's office for not wearing a tie.

PROBLEM 2: Homework

For advice on how to turn this to your advantage, please refer to my earlier book, *Help! My Family is Driving Me Crazy!* Here are a few brief revision notes:

1) The homework excuse. This is invaluable when your parent is nagging you to tidy your room, or anything else you would rather not do. You simply say, "But, Mum, I've got to do my maths homework or Mr Prenderghastly will murder me!" The very notion of Mr Prenderghastly murdering her precious darling will be enough to persuade the tidiest of mothers that it is more important that you get on with your homework.

THE HOMEWORK EXCUSE

2) You can tell your parents that you are working on a project with a friend, and that it is important that the two of you should do your homework together. This gives you an opportunity to get together with your friend for a gossip, a flick through some magazines, a chance to listen to a new tape and, of course, you can do your homework together.

3) Remember to keep your homework diary up to date so that you know what you should be doing. Your parent may want to see this from time to time (they will have been told of its existence), and then they will have a clearer idea of what you haven't been doing. Try to keep on top of your homework so that it doesn't get on top of you. If you fall too far behind, you will find that all your friends are moving on while you stay where you are, stranded.

4) Do you have what IT takes?

The scene

Angelica is able to make use of her father's ultra-sophisticated personal computer, which means that she can access all kinds of useful information to help her with her homework. (Her father also has an ISP – not that he talks about it much – known as a Browser, with full Internet access, which gives Angelica access to all sorts of utterly useless information.) In fact, the computer does her homework for her. She asks it for information on soil erosion, about which she is meant to write an essay for geography, and it produces a beautifully laid-out, four-page document on the subject of soil erosion. There doesn't seem any point in copying it out, so she downloads the entire article, prints it out, and hands it in to Mr Fogg, just as it is. Mr Fogg hands it straight back to her. For some reason, Mr Fogg does not seem very pleased. Why is this?

● **Main reason why Mr Fogg is not pleased:** He wants Angelica to use her brain so that she understands properly what soil erosion is all about. Angelica has not used her brain at all, since the computer has done all the work for her.

● **Helpful hint:** Information technology is there to help you. The tactful thing is to copy out the information you have gained in your own handwriting. The act of writing it out should help to instil it into your brain, and you may even add some thoughts or draw some conclusions of your own.

A special note to sufferers of PMT:

This is short for Pre-Maths Tension. If you are totally numerate and cool with cubed roots (this is not the same as diced carrot), then skip this section, since it does not apply to you. It is sometimes argued that anyone can do maths, but the reason many people cannot handle it is because they are afraid of it. (Or in the case of diced carrot, it makes them sick.) This does not seem to make much sense (did you have a traumatic experience in early life, involving maths? No, but I did have one involving diced carrot.) Here are a few suggested remedies for dealing with Pre-Maths Tension:

1) Try to relax and take it slowly. Make sure you understand what you are trying to do, and don't be afraid to admit it if you don't. Go and see a teacher before or after the lesson if you're embarrassed to do so in front of your mates.

2) If your maths homework makes no sense whatsoever, write "I do not understand this" somewhere in the margin, and then go and take a long and luxurious, foaming herbal bath. This will not help you with your maths, but at least you will be very clean, relaxed and smelling wonderful.

3) Take a deep breath and count to ten. If you are unable to count to ten, it is time you gave up.

Good and bad reasons for not doing your homework:

1) "The dog ate it." This is a good reason if the dog really did eat it. You are likely to be told to keep your homework out of the dog's reach in future or, alternatively, feed the poor animal so that it doesn't have to resort to eating your schoolbooks.

2) "The dog ate it." This is a bad reason if it is the tenth time in three weeks that the dog has consumed your work. Your teacher may begin to smell a rat (rather than a dog).

THIS EXCUSE MAY WEAR A BIT THIN IF IT IS THE TENTH TIME IN THREE WEEKS THAT THE DOG HAS EATEN YOUR HOMEWORK.

3) "The hamster ate it." It could be any animal, of course. Hamsters are voracious eaters, capable of chewing their way through a car's electric wiring loom. Goats eat anything, and are particularly fond of textiles. If your teacher knows you live in a flat, she may be surprised to hear that you have a goat. Beware of the more far-fetched excuses.

4) "I went to a Jamsplat concert. I was dead tired by the time I got back, but it was well worth it." This is an extremely bad reason, as your teacher is most unlikely to agree with you. Even Mr Tardis, the trendy one, would argue that Jamsplat concerts and other similar events should be reserved for weekends, leaving plenty of time for more important things, such as history homework.

5) "I wasn't well." This is a good reason, especially if it happens to be true. It should be used sparingly, however, especially if you appear at school every day, glowing with health. It may seem strange to your teacher if you fall ill on a too-regular basis, between the hours of four p.m. and nine a.m., while the rest of the time you are rudely healthy. (You are allowed to be rudely healthy – it is the only form of rudeness tolerated at school.)

6) "I am suffering from THAS (Total Homework Allergy Syndrome)." Warning: if you invent something like this, you will need a letter from the doctor to support it. Your doctor is unlikely to co-operate. A better reason might be to claim to have suspected glandular fever. The word "suspected" lets you off the hook (you could be better the following day and no longer under suspicion). If you have "suspected" anything too often, however, you are more likely to be suspected of not doing your homework.

On the whole, it is probably less complicated to get on and do your homework.

PROBLEM 3: Exams

From time to time the teachers will slap large notices on the doors of especially designated rooms, stating:

QUIET
EXAM IN PROGRESS

● The scene

Amy and the rest of her group are herded into a room and the doors closed behind them. This is all done in strict silence, which is the major requirement under exam conditions. What this means in real terms is that Amy, and everyone else, becomes acutely aware of other noises, such as the click-clack of heels, the scraping of chair legs, the clatter of someone dropping their pencils on the floor, and the sound of several people suffering the most acute coughing fits. In the distance, Amy can hear shrieks and cries from the school playing fields and, somewhere nearer, the chink chink of cups, plates and cutlery being sorted out and stacked in the school canteen.

"You are expected to remain silent throughout this exam," says the teacher, apparently unaware of all the background noise. "Remember that you are working under exam conditions. You have one hour. You may now turn your papers over." She glances behind her at the clock, only to realise it stopped at ten minutes to two, six months ago, and has not yet been fixed. Fortunately, at least ten people in the room are wearing watches which go "beep beep beep" on the hour, every hour, and one of them makes a noise like a cockerel crowing. St Herbert's has been trying to put a ban on these watches but, so far unsuccessfully.

As the exam begins, Amy's mind goes as blank as the sheet of paper on which she is supposed to write.

THE CARETAKER

● **Main question which you may ask yourself at the beginning of exams:** What on earth do I do now? Why am I here? Help! Let me out of here!

● **Most important answer:** Don't panic!

Things to remember during exams:

1) It is only an exam. There are worse things in life. "Just do your best." That is what people say. By the time you reach the end of your school career, you will be sick of hearing them say it.

2) Remember to look straight ahead or down at your paper. If you look to left or right, you may be accused of cheating. But anyone hoping to gain anything by looking at Kevin Winterbotham's answers on their right or Elspeth Hoggins's on their left is in for a grave disappointment.

3) Don't be put off by the sight of someone scribbling away furiously (well, you wouldn't be, would you, since you aren't supposed to be looking), while you have only managed to come up with three words so far. It is quality that matters, not quantity. The furious scribbler is more likely to make careless mistakes and get marks taken off for an untidy and illegible scrawl.

4) People give silly names to exams. Some are called SATS (Standard Assessment Tests). There are some called CATS

(Cognitive Ability Tests). There are probably some called RATS (Really Awful Tests). Whatever they are called, don't let yourself be intimidated by all the formality and jargon. What really matters is whether you have developed a genuine interest in a subject, which will go a long way towards carrying you through an exam.

Non-essential joke . . .

PROBLEM 4: How to get away with work and not seem like a swot

● The scene

Soumik has a guilty secret. He enjoys maths. He is quite good at it and derives a certain amount of satisfaction from filling up maths exercise books with neat diagrams and numbers, all meticulously worked out and mostly correct. If he gets something wrong he is keen to know why so he can get it right the next time. He wants to do well in his maths exam, but he does not wish to be known as a swot. How can he avoid this?

● The wrong approach: Sit right at the front of the class for your favourite subject. Beam up at the teacher. If anyone around you makes a disturbing noise, turn on them furiously and tell them to "Sssh!" Answer every question the teacher asks before anyone else has a chance to. Leap to your feet and sprint to the door to open it for the teacher when they leave or enter the room. If they forget to set you any homework, remind them. This is how to lose all your friends and become known as a SUPERSWOT (or worse).

● A better approach: Work away quietly at your favourite subject(s), but leave time to talk to your friends. Offer to help them if they are having difficulty with a subject which you understand. But don't say, "Oh, but that's easy! That's so obvious! Any fool could . . ." You will make them feel stupid and they won't thank you for it.

Instead, adopt a low-key approach and say something like, "I think it might work if . . ." so that the other person feels that you are working with them, rather than showing off your superior knowledge. They will probably appreciate your help. You will be less of a SWOT and more of a SWOT(NOT).

● **Best approach:** Realise that there is nothing wrong with enjoying your work as long as your attitude is laid-back (you will enjoy it more if you are relaxed, anyway. But not so relaxed that you are asleep). You can drop a sentence like, "Yeah, maths is cool," into a conversation, and then go on talking about your favourite rock band without upsetting anyone. If you rave on about maths the whole time and nothing else, of course, it is different. You alienate-a-mate when you make them feel stupid because they don't happen to share your ability or enthusiasm for a certain subject. It is a matter of keeping things in proportion, making time for work and time for friends and your social life.

Things to remember about work in general:

1) If you adopt an I-hate-work attitude, you are making life immensely difficult for yourself. You will still have to do the work, like everyone else, whether you like it or not, but it will seem twice as hard if you have already decided that you hate it.

2) If you are constantly thinking, "Help! Let me out of

here!" you will have a fairly miserable time, because no one is going to let you out unless you have a very good reason, or a sick note. It is better to make the most of what might seem like a bad situation until it begins to feel like a good situation. Even if you were let out of school, you would most probably still have to work (to earn money), and the work might be less interesting than the subjects you are studying at school.

3) You can learn a lot from your mates, as well as from the teachers, as some of them may have ideas and information to contribute to class discussions which are genuinely interesting and thought-provoking. OK, so it has already been said that thinking is stressful. This mainly applies to boring and negative thoughts. Your brain needs a certain amount of stimulation, otherwise it will become flabby, which is not a nice thought. So you should allow your brain a gentle workout during lessons, and no harm will come to you.

4) When teachers or parents talk about "stretching your mind", it really isn't as painful as it sounds. The most important thing is to keep an open mind, both towards work and towards your mates. Both can get you down at times, but by working through problems and difficulties you achieve a greater understanding and fuller appreciation, whether of a friend or of a subject.

PROBLEM 5: The school report

Here is an excerpt from Steve's school report:

Maths:

Steve keeps complaining that he is suffering from PMT, but I have always understood this to be a girls' complaint.

C2+E3=D-

English:

I am a little concerned that Steve still seems to think that *King Lear* is some kind of rock group.

D-

GOOD/BEST REASON FOR NOT BREAKING THE RULES: YOU MIGHT GET CAUGHT

History:
Steve is a cool dude. But he is no good at history.

E+

French:
Whatever language Steve is speaking, it is certainly not French.

F-

PE:
Steve has made some great leaps forward this term. He can also leap backwards and sideways, and diagonally across the room. I very much regret that he leapt through a window into a flowerbed, and hope that he makes a full recovery.

B+++++++++++

Techno-techno-technology:
I am recommending that additional safety precautions be taken and protective clothing worn if Steve is to continue to join us in the woodwork and metalwork rooms.

F-

Home Economics:
I would be grateful if Steve would refrain, in future, from bringing woodlice into the food preparation area. I have not yet recovered from finding six of them in a freshly baked roll.

HE-

Art:
Steve claims to be heavily influenced by Picasso. His portraits show great originality and frequently have four or more eyes, six ears, three noses and two mouths.

A++

Headmaster's comment:

Once again, Steve has been caught smoking behind the bicycle sheds. St Herbert's intends to take the elementary precaution of installing clear perspex bicycle sheds, which will mean that anyone walking past will be able to see straight through them to whatever is going on behind.
Tee hee.

Steve has no problems with this report. He is only likely to have problems with it when his parents read it. He can take the sting out of the tail of the school report by announcing his intention of staying on at school to study for A levels, and then continue to university to study law. This sounds incredibly sensible and serious, and his parents should be suitably impressed, especially if Steve manages to keep a straight face. The fact that he has so far failed to pass a single exam in anything may be temporarily forgotten in the warm glow of renewed parental hope and aspirations.

The de-stress solution to lessons:

1) Take a travel pack of wet wipes into an exam or difficult lesson. These are especially soothing when wiped across your forehead or your wrists, particularly during a heatwave, which is the traditional time for taking exams.

2) Remember that the scariest of teachers is only human. Try to imagine them at home, patting their dog on the head or tickling their pussy cat under its chin. (If your mind only manages to conjure up an image of them strangling chickens, then you are not employing this tactic the right way.)

3) Keep your cool and be polite and cheerful. This will go some way towards making up for the fact that you have, once again, forgotten to do your history homework.

4) Practise some gentle yoga breathing exercises to lift your spirits and calm them at the same time. There is one which involves breathing in through one nostril and out through the other. You keep one nostril closed with your finger (it is not necessary to stuff your finger up your nostril to do this). It is probably not a good idea to perform this exercise under exam conditions, as it will make your breathing very noisy, especially if you have a cold. Everyone will look round at you to see if you are hyperventilating.

5) Work out a schedule of study and/or essay-writing. Try not to cram. It is very bad for the nerves.

6) If you are working in pairs, try to do your homework with someone who understands the subject better than you. You can pick up some excellent tips.

DE-STRESS IDEA : YOGA

7) An excellent way of de-stressing lessons is to de-stress the teacher. He or she will become stressed if you don't do the work they set you, so it's best to try to keep them calm. For example, if you are going to be late with some homework, try to make sure it's not the same teacher to whom you handed in late homework last time.

In other words, share the load.

CHAPTER 4
Not Work

The two Rs (Rest and Recreation – making five Rs in total, if you add them on to the three R's Reading, 'Riting and 'Rithmetic)

PROBLEM 1: Break-times

The scene

Angelica is moping around the classroom, not sure what to do in the small amount of time before the next bell goes. Suddenly she says, "Oh, I'm so ugly!" Amy is the only other person in the room at the time. What should she say?

Bad thing to say: "Yes, you certainly are!"

Slightly better thing to (not) say: Nothing. This is bound to be disconcerting, since Angelica is hoping that Amy will say, "No, you're not!" By saying nothing it seems as if she is agreeing when, in fact, she is neither agreeing nor disagreeing.

Best thing to say: "No, you're not."

Completely stupid conversation which inevitably follows:

"Oh, yes I am. I'm ugly."

"No, you're not. I'm much uglier!"

"No, you're not! You're not ugly at all. But I am."
"No, you're NOT. I AM."

And so on. Fortunately, the bell goes and Amy and Angelica move off in different directions, since they are in different sets for maths, which is the next lesson. This definitely falls into the category of "saved by the bell", and there will be times when you are very glad to hear the bell, especially if you have got into a stupid argument with one of your friends. In Amy and Angelica's case, it is definitely better not to fish for compliments, because it will be very damaging to the ego if you fail to get any, and you are almost bound to irritate-a-mate. Find something more constructive to do with your time, such as decorating the cover of a folder with pictures cut from a favourite magazine and swapped with friends for even better ones (it helps you get through double physics if you can gaze at the dark and handsome features of Matt Moody, smouldering up at you from your folder).

On other occasions you will not be at all pleased to hear the bell signalling the end of break-time, because you are enjoying yourself so much. It is annoying if you have joined one of the lunch-time clubs such as trampolining, and you were just about to bounce higher than you have ever bounced in your life before: the ringing of the bell brings you down to earth with a bump and you remember, with a sinking feeling, that you have forgotten to write the essay you were supposed to, entitled "What is a tragic hero?" (You are.)

SAVED BY THE BELL

Good things and bad things about break-time:

- **Good thing:** You can go to the canteen.

- **Bad thing:** You get stuck in a queue in the canteen, and by the time you get to the front of it someone has just bought the last Danish pastry, which was the only thing you felt like (at least you don't look like one – try to look on the bright side).

- **Another good thing:** You can go to the library and sit and read a book, quietly (yes, this really IS a good thing, especially if you happen to be the studious and thoughtful type, like Mark Bookmark).

- **An equally bad thing:** You find that a great crowd of people has converged on the library, making loads of noise and fooling around with the photocopier on the pretext of doing something serious. (Mr Trusscott, the head, decides later that day to introduce a secret code so that no one can use the photocopier without special permission. Bear in mind that if you abuse privileges, and it is indeed a privilege to operate a photocopier, then they will inevitably get taken away.)

- **Another thing:** If you are desperate you can retire to the loos with your book for some peace and quiet. But mind the loo seat. And holding your nose while reading a book makes it difficult to relax anyway.

● **Another bad thing:** You may find yourself in the corridor, face to face with someone you would rather not see – perhaps you have borrowed one of their favourite tapes and not returned it (because your dog ate it).

● **A good/bad thing:** There is such a crush, noise, jostle and kerfuffle (to name but four things) in the corridor, that it is relatively easy to avoid someone you would rather not see and slip away through the crowd to another part of the building. However, it is also quite annoying to get continually jostled and pushed when you are trying to have an important conversation with someone. It doesn't seem quite right to have to yell at the top of your voice, "MUM SAYS IT'S INFECTIOUS AND YOU OUGHT TO SEE THE DOCTOR IMMEDIATELY!" You may find that suddenly everything goes quiet and everyone is staring at you. If you need to have a confidential talk with someone, it is probably better to find a quiet corner (such as the far end of the playing fields).

● **A suggestion:** A good way of getting some peace and quiet during break-time would be to volunteer yourself and a few friends to tidy up the classroom. This buys you some peace and quiet, a few brownie points from the teacher and, if there are enough of you, you might get away with not being labelled as teacher's pet. This is also a good way of staying warm in cold weather as a bad point about breaks is that some schools like to enforce fresh air on the pupils (particularly good if your school is in an industrial area or adjacent to a busy road with constant traffic thundering by). You are forced to stand shivering in the yard, hugging the corners of buildings to stay out of the wind and bitterly regretting your decision to make your skirt even shorter. Some more enlightened schools have "wet-weather rooms", although not many have "overcast-with-the-threat-of-light-drizzle rooms" or "slightly-breezy rooms".

PROBLEM 2: Sports

You could argue that sports definitely fall into the category of work (and hard work, certainly, as you struggle round the muddy perimeter of the playing fields for the eighth time on a cross country run). You can even take a GCSE in PE. (If you can say, "I'm studying for my PEGCSE," and get the letters in the right order, you deserve to pass.)

BUT DON'T FORGET: Sport is meant to be FUN. In reality, it often falls a little short of full-blown fun.

● The scene

Angelica hates hockey. She hunches miserably down the far end of the hockey pitch in the left back or right back position. In her opinion, it is not nearly far enough back; she would willingly settle for "right back off the playing field" or "back in the classroom/canteen". Sometimes she lurks in the showers for the entire lesson, but today she has been dragged unwillingly on to the pitch by her friend Amy, an enthusiastic hockey player. Suddenly Angelica

BEWARE OF BELINDA BOSSINGTON-HOCKEYBOOTS!

notices Belinda Bossington-Boots and Beverley McBrisk bearing down on her, hockey sticks aloft, both in pursuit of a very hard ball which is hurtling towards her at break-ankle speed. Angelica's instinct is for self-preservation, so she turns and runs. Beverley McBrisk scores a goal, the whistle blows and Amy and Angelica's team loses the match. A furious Belinda Bossington-Boots grabs Angelica by the shoulder and hisses furiously at her, "How could you be so STUPID?" Angelica is rather shaken by this incident. Back in the changing rooms she sits forlornly in a corner, wondering why she feels depressed. It is because she has just encountered . . .

The person who takes competitive sport extremely seriously:
This kind of person treats a hockey/Rugby/football/basketball/netball/softball match as a matter of life and death. The most important thing is to WIN at all costs, and they just can't stand it if they lose. They have to blame someone, and their anger seems out of proportion. They fume and fulminate (good word, this), and it is a good idea to keep out of their way until the dust has settled. (It is also a good idea to check the rule book to see if fulminating is

allowed at your school.) This kind of person is often rather intense and, at times, lacking in sense of humour.

How should Angelica handle the situation?

● **Good thing to do:** Leave Belinda Bossington-Boots well alone. Any attempt to apologise to her will wind her up even further, and it should really be Belinda herself who should be apologising to Angelica for being so nasty to her. She may even do this, given time to calm down.

● **Even better thing to do:** Angelica should join her friends, who will do a lot to cheer her up. Amy is a keen hockey player, but regards her friendships as being far more important than any sport could ever be. Right now she is doubled up with mirth at the memory of Angelica turning and running away from the ball.

● **The moral of this tale:** If you are seriously over-competitive you will take all the fun out of sport, and are likely to alienate-a-mate on a fairly regular basis. The more laid back you are in your attitude to competitive sport, the more likely you are to enjoy it (it is the taking part that matters, not the winning, and the British have always admired a good loser. In fact, it has become a fine tradition in Britain to lose at sport – though there are exceptions, of course). You can, however, be too laid back, like Steve, who regards chasing any kind of ball around as a futile waste of time and energy. He prefers to stand still and wait till the ball comes to him. It does, occasionally,

and he usually misses it. You won't have any fun, either, if you are not prepared to join in to a certain extent.

The scene

Soumik is not very keen on sport, but he loves wearing all

the right gear, including Reeboks, shorts and T-shirts adorned with trendy labels such as Adidas and Lacoste, with matching sweatshirt and jogging bottoms, a gum shield, which he likes to wear not because he is a keen Rugby player (he dislikes getting mud on his smart socks and Rugby jersey), but in order to look macho.

There is a word for Soumik: POSER. He doesn't mind being called a poser by his friends, as long as he gets plenty of admiring looks from the girls. One day he notices that Baz is looking fed up. "What's up?" he asks.

SPOT THE POSER

"I wish I could afford some new trainers," Baz replies. "I look a complete prat standing next to you."

Is this true?

● **Answer:** No. Just because Baz cannot afford all the right gear does not mean no girl will look at him. In fact, the reverse may even be true. Soumik's starched, crisp, freshly ironed and worn-for-the-first-time appearance speaks of rather too much maternal input. When Baz plays Rugby in his torn old shirt and scruffy shorts, rotten old socks and second-hand boots, he gets covered in mud. There is something quite attractively male about this, as long as you do not get too near to it when wearing your best white top.

It is only fair to say that when Soumik plays cricket there is usually a small crowd of female admirers, so startlingly white are his cricket whites. Mrs Sen, Soumik's mother, takes her job of caring for Soumik's sports kit and the rest of his uniform extremely seriously. If you are not fortunate enough to have this kind of dedicated mother, you could at least remember to put your sports kit through the wash once a month (the smell of sweaty socks in the changing rooms is pungent, which is probably the politest word to describe it, and it certainly rivals the smell in the school loos as a Smell To Remember For The Rest Of Your Life).

PROBLEM 3: A musical interlude

● The scene - 1

Sometimes you've just got to blow your own trumpet, meaning that you have to stand up and show the world what you've got, and blow what you've got for all you're worth, if it happens to be a trumpet or something similar. In Kevin Winterbotham's case it is a tuba. The rest of his year wishes that Kevin and his tuba would go somewhere else (anywhere else), but it is not possible for Kevin and his tuba (both of whom are rather large) to fit into one of the very small music practice rooms. Kevin has tried practising in the school hall, but the noise was very off putting to someone trying to work out a complicated piece on the piano at the same time, and also disturbed the concentration of a group of jazz dancers working on a dance routine. Most of Kevin's year is rehearsing for a concert to be performed in front of the school and a number of specially invited guests.

What Kevin has achieved so far:

Apart from emptying the room he is currently in, he has managed to force a few strangled-duck noises out of his tuba, and a deeper sound, which most closely resembles a hippopotamus farting (once heard, never forgotten). What should Kevin do?

● **Not the right thing to do:** Give up. It is too easy to be put off by other people's reactions and the fact that other people can do things better than you can. This is always going to be the case throughout your life, and it is not a good reason for giving up. The important thing is that you should derive some pleasure from whatever hobby/musical instrument/other recreational activity you have chosen, and the enjoyment you get out of it should communicate itself to others. Playing a musical instrument or listening to music has always been a wonderful way to relax and to de-stress. Kevin and his tuba just happen to be an exception to this rule. But it is possible they will succeed as a comic turn and end up the stars of the show as a result.

● **Best thing to do:** Throw yourself into it (although it is probably best if Kevin does not throw himself into his tuba, as he is likely to get stuck).

● **Fact:** If you are taking part in a school concert, the turn immediately before you will almost certainly be the most brilliant and gifted musician in the school, recent winner of numerous scholarships, who will give a virtuoso performance on the violin and repeated encores to rapturous applause. Fifteen minutes later, when the last of the clapping has finally died away, you are sent on with your flute to play a staccato version of *Frère Jacques*. Your flute behaves more like a toot, ending with a shrill and piercing squeak which causes everyone's eyebrows to rise and their ears to twitch. Never mind. You did it. That is the most important thing.

The scene - 2

Mr Baton, the music teacher, insists that everyone must sing, whether in assembly or choir or during his lessons. An inability to hit the right note (or any note) is no excuse as far as he is concerned, and he has a seemingly endless repertoire of dreadful and embarrassing songs, which he expects his pupils to sing. Baz feels totally uncool as he stands up with the others to sing "The Fiddlestone Tree":

Sing high, sing low,
Sing hey nonny no,
Sing wild, sing free,
Jolly forest folk we,
Join hands and dance
Round the Fiddlestone Tree.

This is only the chorus, and there are ten verses of complete rubbish (as far as Baz is concerned). Baz has no idea what a Fiddlestone Tree is, but he is certain he would never do anything quite as uncool as dance round it, and there is a definite shortage of trees where he lives, so he feels very far from being a "jolly forest person". He might just qualify for "jolly depressed, non-forest person", as his mother has been giving him a very hard time recently. And, this morning, one of the goldfish decided to turn up its toes and die which, for some reason, reduced his mother to tears (Baz has never felt particularly close to the goldfish).

Suddenly he is aware that Mr Baton is shouting at him: "Shoulders back, Basil! Open your mouth and give it some oomph! 'The Fiddlestone Tree' must be sung lustily!" Lustily? Baz is quite happy to lust after Gina, the gorgeous girl in year twelve, but it seems an inappropriate word to apply to such a completely naff song. It is certainly inappropriate to the way he's feeling. He doesn't feel inclined to discuss his problems with Mr Baton, who has no sympathy with people who do not open their mouths and "give it some oomph". How can Baz survive the rest of the lesson?

Stupid school song survival strategies:

1) Suggest to your teacher that you and your friends could choose a song for yourselves (or maybe even compose one

Non-essential joke . . .

SCHOOL RULE : NO EATING IN THE CORRIDORS

of your own) and sing it to him or her. An up-to-date, go-ahead sort of teacher would probably welcome such an enterprising attitude, whereas a more old-fashioned teacher might not appreciate any disagreement with their own choice of song ("The Fiddlestone Tree" is one of Mr Baton's personal favourites).

2) Soften up an unwilling teacher first by showing some enthusiasm for their choice of music. (You know how boring it is when adults dismiss your music as tuneless noise without even bothering to listen to it properly. All they can say is "Turn it down!" So imagine how your poor music teacher must feel when everyone makes it obvious that they hate his or her songs.) Soften them up first – give the most excruciatingly awful song as much oomph as you can – and THEN suggest that you choose your own.

3) If you can't sing, pretend to sing along. You will have to hope that your friends will make up for your lack of voice.

4) Develop a terrible coughing fit so that you have to leave the room. This will work once or twice, but you can't cough your way through the whole of your school career. At least, it's inadvisable. Your teacher may also get suspicious if nearly the whole class ends up in the corridor, coughing their heads off.

PROBLEM 4: Drama. A class act

● The scene

The Farmer Wants a Wife
a short play by
Steve Cash and Amy Average

Act One:

THE FARMER (Steve): Ooooooo-ARRR!

(This immediately gets a laugh and Mrs Macbeth, the drama teacher, has to tell everyone to be quiet so that they can get on with it.)

THE FARMER: Ooooooo-ARRR!

(The whole class collapses in quivering heaps of hysterical laughter. Mrs Macbeth loses her cool at this point and gives a good practical demonstration of how to interpret the emotion of anger. It is, however, a good idea to be able to distinguish between the times when your drama teacher is acting and when he or she is not. It does not go down at all well when Soumik gives Mrs Macbeth a round of applause and says, "That was amazing, Mrs Macbeth! You've even managed to go red in the face! I wish I could act like you."

Mrs Macbeth exercises self-control, and the play continues.)

THE FARMER: I am a very lonely farmer. I only have my cows, sheep, pigs and chickens for company.

ANIMALS (Amy): Moo, baa, oink, cluck.

(More sounds of barely suppressed laughter from the audience.)

MRS MACBETH (as herself): Isn't that rather childish? Can we have a little more focus on character and plot, please?

THE FARMER: I am a lonely and sad character, and I have a small plot of land.

MRS MACBETH: That was not quite what I meant.

THE FARMER: I want a wife.

MRS MACBETH: Isn't that a rather bald statement? What has led up to the farmer wanting a wife? How does the farmer actually feel? Can you make us feel what the farmer feels?

THE FARMER: WILL YOU PLEASE STOP

INTERRUPTING? I'm sorry, Mrs Macbeth, but I can't concentrate!

MRS MACBETH: That was quite good, Steve. A little more emotion, that's what we need.

THE FARMER: I WANT A WIFE!

THE CHORUS (Baz, Soumik and Angelica): *The farmer wants a wife, The farmer wants a wife, Hey ho . . .*

MRS MACBETH: Yes, yes. Can we move on to the main action, please?

(The chorus sits down.)

THE FARMER: What a beautiful girl! She has come to collect the eggs and take them to market. But I dare not talk to her. I am an ugly old farmer in a stupid hat, with a stupid beard. She won't be interested in me.

BEAUTIFUL GIRL (Amy): What a handsome farmer! I really like his hat and his beard. But I am too shy to talk to him.

(There is a very long dramatic pause during which the farmer plucks up the necessary courage to ask the beautiful girl to marry him. She says yes. Shortly afterwards, a child appears on the scene (Soumik), followed by a dog (Baz).

The play ends with everyone patting the dog, and the audience is invited to participate. Mrs Macbeth has a certain amount of difficulty getting the audience to return to their seats, but she has to admit that the play has been a great success, even though the characters were not fully (or at all) developed and there was a notable absence of plot.

Good things about drama:

1) If you have recently had a row or are feeling tense, angry or stressed in some way, you can let rip in front of the whole class, giving vent to some of your pent-up emotions by throwing yourself into whatever part you have been given and overacting madly. You can swing your arms about wildly, raise your voice, even throw yourself on to the floor (look out for dropped drawing pins), all in the name of drama. All of this is more difficult, of course, if you have been given the part of a tree (although a tree in a high wind can wave its branches about wildly, go "WHOOOOSH!" and be blown down on to the ground). It is certainly more difficult if your only line is, "Yes, sir. I have put the luggage in the boot."

2) With any luck you will have a drama teacher who encourages self-expression and provides opportunities for you to express yourself. If you find it difficult to do this, especially in front of an audience, you can learn a lot from watching other people. No one minds if you make (in your opinion) a complete fool of yourself, since everyone else is doing the same thing, and you are all in it together.

3) Not everyone can act. Not everyone wants to. But there are plenty of opportunities for doing things backstage: helping with costumes, make-up and scenery, and learning stage management and production skills.

4) You can write plays, on your own or with friends.

DRAMA – A CLASS ACT
(OR HOW TO MOVE YOUR TEACHER TO TEARS)

5) Drama provides a good way into the study of set texts. Acting out *King Lear* or any other play, or seeing it on stage, helps bring it to life.

6) Theatre and film expeditions to see important productions are usually interesting and exciting and they get you out of school. Don't expect your drama teacher to take you to *School Terminator III*, starring Arnie Musclemaker and Sigourney Silicon-implant, no matter how rave the reviews have been. You are more likely to be taken to the film version of *Romeo and Juliet* (which is actually very good).

7) You can write about the plays you have seen at school for the school review. Don't take yourself too seriously as a film or theatre critic or you may alienate-a-mate. Examples of bad reviews:

I found Jamie Pennington's production of I Was a Teenage Pizza Fanatic *particularly tedious, and the fact that it was based on Jamie's real-life experiences did nothing to recommend it to me. Mind-numbing stuff.*

Harry Harrison's performance in the school production of Pinball Pinochio *was wooden in the extreme. Mrs Macbeth was definitely having an off-day when she wrote this play. The characters were not at all developed and there was a notable absence of plot.*

Bad things about drama:

Confusing drama with real life.

The scene

Angelica is not keen on acting, whereas her friend Amy is an aspiring actress. Amy is delighted when she is cast as Juliet opposite Harry Harrison as Romeo. Harry Harrison is something of a school heart-throb.

"I even get to do a stage kiss with him!" enthuses Amy. "Just think about it, Jel (short for Angelica), he has to put his arms round me. Oh, wow!"

Angelica *is* thinking about it. She is aware of feeling acutely jealous, since she has fancied Harry Harrison for ages and admired him from a distance. This makes her feel guilty, since she ought to be feeling pleased for Amy. It is Amy's big break. What should she say?

● **Wrong thing to say:** "Big deal. What's so special about Harry Harrison, anyway? The whole thing's a yawn." Putting everything and everyone down like this will certainly alienate-a-mate. It also makes it more obvious that you are upset, and you will feel worse for adopting a negative attitude.

● **Better thing to say:** "That's great, Amy. Really great. Terrific." (Try to sound as though you mean it.) Just because Harry and Amy are Romeo and Juliet on stage doesn't mean they are suddenly going to fall in love in real life. This is unlikely, since Harry already has a steady girlfriend and a string of admirers, of which Amy and Angelica are just two.

● **Best thing to say:** "Oh, wow! You lucky thing! I really envy you – but you deserve it, you've worked so hard and you're great at acting." In other words, be honest about your feelings but keep the situation light-hearted and in perspective. You could offer to help backstage in order to get closer to the person you admire and to join in the buzz and excitement of a major production. If you are genuinely pleased for your friend and their achievement, they will be pleased for you when your turn comes, as it surely will (Angelica is brilliant at home economics and food technology, and wins first prize at a local "food fayre" for the Most Outstanding Cake. She is interviewed for the local television news by an outstandingly dishy reporter.)

Celebrate success – but don't let it go to your head. Beware of being a stage-struck shooting star who considers himself or herself to be God's gift to members of the opposite sex just because they have played Romeo or Juliet on stage to a standing ovation. They are definitely in danger of confusing real life with acting.

The de-stress solutions for Rest and Recreation:

1) Take your Walkman to school so that you can listen to your favourite music, but not during lessons. Mr Tardis, the trendy one, may give you permission to use it during his lesson if you argue that listening to Jamsplat helps you concentrate. Or, more likely, he may borrow it so that he can listen to it himself.

2) Meanwhile, back at the canteen, you can relax with a nice cup of tea (it is difficult to relax with a nasty cup of tea). You may prefer a can of Coke or an orange juice. It is important to replace lost body fluids after sweating like a pig on the school playing fields doing the triple jump (hop, step and jump or, in Steve's case, hop, trip and splat).

3) It is relaxing to put your feet up, but don't take this too

literally in the canteen or in the classrooms. The dinner ladies tend to frown on people putting their feet on the tables. Most teachers object when they look out at the class and are confronted by the soles of several people's trainers staring back at them.

In certain cultures it is a most dreadful insult to point the soles of your feet at someone, and you can understand why when they are encased in a dreadful pair of smelly old sweaty socks or mouldy old trainers. Have some consideration. Your socks could severely stress someone's nose.

4) Don't tilt your chair back in your desire to stretch out and relax. If the chair goes over backwards you could end up with a back injury which will cause you a great deal of distress. Distress is not a good way to de-stress.

5) It is supposed to be particularly relaxing and good for you to elevate your legs so your feet are above your head. You could try doing this during Mr Prenderghastly's maths lesson and explain to him that you are trying to resemble an obtuse angle. You can explain to any other teacher that the extra supply of blood to your brain will help you to get on with your work. When your face turns as red as a ripe tomato, you may conclude that enough blood has reached your head (don't elevate for too long).

CHAPTER 5 "I am unwell."

PROBLEM 1: Too sick to go to school

The scene

Steve is suffering from PMT again (Pre-Maths Tension). He is also feeling distinctly bruised after his fall through a window into a flowerbed full of the sort of prickly and spiny bushes beloved of school garden planners, and then, having more or less recovered from that, his dramatic trip, followed by a whole body drop, face down in the sand during the triple jump. He is still having to pick the sand out of his nostrils. The final straw is the ominous feeling that he has a cold coming on (or maybe it is just sand on the tonsils). This is undoubtedly a long list of

SICK DURING A LESSON – DON'T BE SURPRISED IF YOUR TEACHER DOESN'T NOTICE THAT YOU LOOK ANY DIFFERENT FROM THE WAY YOU USUALLY DO

ailments, any one of which Steve considers sufficient grounds for missing school.

But are his tutor, year head or any of the other teachers likely to agree with his self diagnosis?

● **Answer:** Not really.

● **What can Steve do?** He must produce a sick note to support his case and take it with him to school next time he goes. Unfortunately, his mother is too busy to write sick notes and his father is totally unsympathetic, with a tendancy to make uncalled for remarks along the lines of "Namby-pamby, molly-coddled wimps," and "Bring back National Service, that's what I say!" But he is too busy wrestling with the huge amount of paper emerging from his Port-o-fax to take much notice of Steve. Steve wonders what to do next.

● **Inspired (probably not) idea:** Steve decides to forge a sick note as follows:

> Dear Mr Truscot Mr Prenderghostly Mrs Spottiswood the school nurse and anyone else to whom it might be of concern to,
>
> My beluved son Steve is gravely ill I fear so I have called the doctor who wishes to say sumthing I'll just pass this letter over to him here you are doc over to you.
>
> Thanx Mrs Cash may I call you Anthea yes it looks too me as tho your son

> Steve has scarlit fever and inlarged tonsoles to name but two reasons why he should stay home and rest and stay away from school in case he infex people thanx Anthea may I borrow your pen I'll just sign my name here goes
>
> Signed Dr O'Dreary Dr. O'Dreary
>
> and Anthea Cash A Cash

Steve types all this out on his mother's computer so that it looks very smart. He runs the spellcheck programme on it and it rejects most of the letter, offering a varied selection of outrageous alternatives. Steve pulls a face. The computer is clearly round the bend. But he is pleased with the letter, particularly with the name he has chosen for the doctor and the clever way in which he has forged his mother's signature. He puts the letter in one of his mother's scented, floral envelopes and takes it into school six days later when he feels well enough to return.

● **The likely effect of Steve's letter on Mr Trusscott, the headmaster:** Mr Trusscott decides to bring forward the scheduled date for his early retirement. In the meantime, Steve receives a quiet summons to the head's office and the door closes behind him. Half an hour later, Steve emerges looking a lot more ill than he has ever looked in his life before. He has no further absences for the rest of the term.

Moral of this tale: If you are tempted to skive off school, remember that it is yourself you will be harming in the long run, as you will fall further and further behind with your work, and you will miss out on the company of your friends while you are stuck at home in full lounge-lizard or couch-potato mode.

PROBLEM 2: Sick during a lesson (or how to get out of games or double maths)

The scene

Angelica cannot face the thought of a cross-country run, so she suddenly drops on to one knee in front of Mrs Hurdleston, the games teacher, and emits a cry of pain: "Aargh! My knee! I think it's dislocated! Look – the kneecap's gone over to one side. That's really scary, Mrs Hurdleston – what if my kneecap slips right round to the back?"

Mrs Hurdleston looks sceptical. She cannot afford to take any risks, however, as she might incur the wrath of parents, doctors, knee specialists and head teachers alike. With a sigh, she tells Angelica to return to the changing rooms. Angelica is triumphant. But she should refrain from doing a victory leap into the air and shouting, "Yay!" since Mrs Hurdleston may begin to smell a rat. Mrs Hurdleston may smell an even bigger rat when Angelica turns up later that same day to take part in the annual maradance, an all-night aerobic dancing event to raise money for school funds.

What can Angelica say to get herself off the hook? "Hi, Mrs Hurdleston! My knee's much better now, all thanks to you for letting me rest this afternoon! I really wanted it to be better so I could take part in the maradance. It's really important to me to help raise money for the school."

Mrs Hurdleston may even feel tempted to believe Angelica, if she is this polite and charming.

Good excuses/reasons for girls to get out of games or other lessons:

1) Period pains (but you are only allowed to have these once a month. If you have them every week, you may find yourself referred to a specialist).

2) Headaches. A full-blown migraine will get you out of lessons for longer, or even sent home.

3) Knee injury.

4) Fainting.

5) Emotional upset (but don't expect too much sympathy if you are still grieving for a pet gerbil which died six months ago. It has to be relatively serious).

DODGY WAY TO GET OUT OF LESSONS

Good excuses/reasons for boys to get out of games or other lessons:

1) Stomach ache. Grumbling appendix. (But NOT, "It's the time of the month, sir.")

2) Headache. Cluster headache sounds more serious and may get you out of double physics. Or go for a migraine.

3) Knee injury.

REASONS FOR GETTING OUT OF LESSONS: EMOTIONAL UPSET (THIS ONE IS MORE DIFFICULT IF YOU ARE A 17 STONE RUGBY PLAYER).

4) Shin injury. You will be told off for not wearing shin pads.

5) Groin injury (footballers only. Rugby players are expected to continue playing, no matter how many injuries they have. A blow to the head, which makes you see double, may get you carted off to hospital, but it is not recommended, even to get out of double French).

6) Fainting (again, this is more convincing if you are a sensitive type, interested in the arts, rather than a great hulking Rugby player).

7) Emotional problems (sorry, this one's not for Rugby players, either).

8) But don't be surprised if it is the biggest, baddest rugby player who passes out while waiting in the queue outside the sick bay for his BCG injection.

The de-stress solution:

1) All things considered, it is probably better not to be ill. Make sure you get plenty of rest, eat properly, relax and stay cool (as opposed to having a raging temperature, which is no fun at all).

2) You should certainly avoid crying wolf too many times or no one will believe you when you really are ill. Also, getting out of lessons is one thing, but getting into them

Non-essential joke . . .

again may be stressful, since you will have fallen behind the rest of the class and will probably be given extra work to do in order to catch up.

3) What happens when you have got out of a lesson? Is it really less stressful to sit in the sick bay like a lemon (a sick lemon) waiting for a stressed/anxious parent who has been called away from their work to come and take you home? They, like the school nurse, may subject you to awkward questions, such as, "Have you been eating properly?" (I had a chocolate bar for breakfast.) "Too many late nights, possibly?" (Possibly.) "You don't look ill. Are you sure you're not feeling well?" (Er, I think I'm beginning to feel a bit better. I think I may be able to struggle through the rest of the day . . .) "Well, we'd better get you to the doctor for a full check-up, just in case. He'll probably take some blood to make sure you're not anaemic. And he'll want a urine sample. You know what to do with this little container?" (ACTUALLY, I'M FINE NOW. IN FACT, I'VE NEVER FELT BETTER IN MY LIFE. CAN I GO NOW, PLEASE? I'M MISSING DOUBLE BIOLOGY!).

To sum up:

Be cool. Stay in school.

CHAPTER 6 School Trips

PROBLEM 1: The day trip

The scene - 1

Amy is going on a techno-techno-technology day trip with the textiles group to see a fashion show in a large local town. The fashion show is not due to begin until two p.m., which leaves two hours to explore the town. Miss Tiedye, the textiles teacher, tells Amy and Angelica and their friends to meet her back outside the town hall at a quarter to two. Amy and Angelica have a wonderful time trying on clothes in various boutiques, and Amy buys a wraparound skirt and a crop top. Angelica buys some make-up. Then they phone Amy's mum from a phone booth and tell her what a great time they're having going round the shops. She sounds a little taken aback. "Er, aren't you meant to be at a fashion show?" she says.

"Oh, wow! Is that the time?" exclaims Angelica, just as the town-hall clock strikes two. They make a mad dash and arrive at the fashion show with seconds to spare. The fashion show is quite interesting, but the most memorable and worthwhile things about this trip were, of course, the shopping and the getting out of lessons.

Things to remember on any school trip:

1) If you fool around too much or get into trouble with the locals (for rollerblading round MacDonalds or the

DON'T ROLLERBLADE ON THE ROMAN REMAINS

Roman remains, for instance), you will not be taken on any further school trips and you will be stuck with double chemistry on a Wednesday afternoon for what seems like the rest of your life.

2) You can claim that your trip round the shops was in order to compare and contrast different kinds of material, and you can even take notes to this effect. Amy and Angelica show Miss Tiedye the crimson Lycra crop top and the purple wraparound mini-skirt they bought in the Cool Clothing Company.

"These are examples of the different kinds of textiles which are available in many different colours. We have conducted a great deal of in-depth research in the last two hours and have come to the conclusion that we could do with another two hours, at least, to complete our research. How about, it Miss Tiedye?"

But don't be surprised if the school bursar/finance director refuses to fork out for a year nine shopping trip.

3) Remember all the things you need, such as pencils, a plastic bag in case you're sick on the coach, a hat to keep the sun/rain off, tissues, lip salve, mobile phone, and so on.

4) You will be given a clipboard, and whenever a teacher walks past, you should give the appearance of studying something intently and making copious notes.

5) Bear in mind that this kind of hands-on, out-in-the-field, in-touch-with-it-all kind of experience should certainly go a long way to bringing the subject in question to life. This is particularly true of a science field trip to the sort of museum/exhibition which has working models, experiments and displays which you can activate by pressing buttons.

6) A maths field trip would be rather less interesting. You would probably be expected to measure the perimeter of the field, examine its angles, and then bisect it by walking straight across it, until you trip over a tussock (not to be confused with a hummock – or a hassock which is a cross between the two) and fall flat on your face in a cowpat. This would be the original kind of field trip, involving, as

it would, a visit to an actual field. Not wildly exciting. You would have to watch out for bulls.

The scene - 2

Soumik and the rest of his history group are visiting the enormous cathedral of St Sigismund in the centre of bustling Borechester. They are all meant to be following an official guide, who is explaining the historical significance of parts of the building. Soumik becomes fascinated by a very large spider which is climbing up one of the stone pillars leading up to the enormously high vaulted ceiling. He watches to see how far the spider will get. Just as it is about to reach a stone arch, it falls off and disappears down behind one of the pews. When Soumik looks round, the rest of his group has disappeared and he is unable to find them among all the crowds. What should he do?

● **Wrong thing to do:** Shout at the top of your voice to your mates, "HEY, STEVO! JEZ! BAZ! WHERE ARE YOU, GUYS?" Shouting like this is likely to annoy most people near you and get you into trouble. This is especially likely to be the case in a cathedral or other large building, because your voice will echo in a most impressive way (your teachers will NOT be impressed). It is an equally bad idea to shout in a museum/library or any other enclosed space where people are quietly looking at things. It is also unwise to shout if you are somewhere in the mountains where you might set off an avalanche or rock fall.

● **Better thing to do:** Keep your cool. Don't panic. On the other hand, don't be tempted to wander off on your own and not bother about the rest of the school trip. Being lost loses its appeal after a while, and you will be in even deeper trouble when you are eventually found, because everyone will have become worried and thoroughly stressed while searching for you.

Best thing to do: Find an official, if you are at a museum or somewhere similar, and tell them you have become separated from the rest of your group ("become separated" sounds better than "lost"). They will probably be able to point you in the right direction. Or simply go to the main entrance of wherever you happen to be since, sooner or later, the other members of your group will have to go through it.

If you are lost in the middle of a busy town or city centre or in the wilds of Outer Nowhere, and there is no one you particularly feel like asking to tell you the way (don't talk to strangers/cows/sheep etc.), it is best to return to the point at which you began, such as the school coach, and then your teachers and your mates should know where to find you. If you would rather not admit to having got lost (or even "become separated") and wish to avoid stupid comments made at your expense, you could say that you returned to the coach because of a bad headache, or something similar. (You will probably be told by your teacher that you should have reported to him/her first, but at least you avoid losing face in front of your friends.)

Further facts about school trips:

1) Weekend field trips will give you time to visit all sorts of fields and also hills, mountains, moors, rivers and sea shores, all in the space of two days, so be prepared for blisters, knee injuries, the occasional drenching in a sudden downpour of rain, followed by your nose turning red either as a result of the freezing conditions or the scorching sun.

2) Take sun cream, cold cream, cream of tomato soup in a thermos, insect-bite cream and any other cream which seems appropriate under the circumstances.

3) The overseas trip can be a nightmare if you find yourself crossing the Channel by ferry during a force ten gale. The French teacher, Mr Fotherington, is a fresh air fiend (which is why he preferred to travel to France above ground rather than below), but this is rather too much fresh air even for him, and he lies on his bunk groaning quietly for the entire crossing. Nearly everyone is sick.

4) The overseas trip can also be a nightmare if the rowdy elements among your number misbehave in the town where you are staying. Mr Fotherington gets a bad headache, trying to remember how many people he has sent into the local *boulangerie*, three at a time, to ask in French for "*Un petit pain, s'il vous plaît.*" He forgets who he has already asked and finds himself explaining to a French boy how to ask in French for a small roll.

5) Going on the ski trip is a good way for Mr Fotherington to recover from the effects of the French trip. He particularly enjoys the *après* ski, but you are meant to concentrate on your skiing. You have to learn how to fall over, which is especially useful for Mr Fotherington, after all the *après* ski.

Interesting fact:
St Herbert's insists on a ratio of one member of staff for every ten pupils going on a school trip. So, for a trip consisting of eighty-five pupils, it is necessary to have eight-and-a-half teachers. Look out for the half-teacher. They may be quite difficult to spot, since they are likely to be quite short, and it is particularly easy to lose them if the field you are visiting has very long grass.

Tips for trips:

1) Write postcards home (this is not necessary if you have only gone on a day trip to the local town). The folks back home will appreciate hearing from you. They like to know you are all right and having a good time. You should avoid writing something like:

Hi, it's me.

The food is grotty. I have an upset stomach and so does everyone else. Wish I wasn't here. I miss you all terribly, even my dear little brother Kevin. Must go now or my tears will smudge the ink. Kiss the dog and Dad,

From Me.

2) Treat the people you meet with courtesy and respect and you will get much more out of your visit, as the local people will warm to you and welcome you into their museum/community/field. If you are out in the wilds and there are no other people around, treat the local cows/caribou/sheep with respect and courtesy, and they will stare at you as if you are mad.

3) Travel light. Perhaps it is not necessary to take two cricket bats, ball and wickets with you to France (learn to play *boule* while you're there, instead), and perhaps you do not need four pairs of stilettos for your surfing holiday off the coast of Cornwall.

4) Visiting a foreign country will undoubtedly help you in your efforts to learn the language, but it is a good idea to pay some attention during the lessons leading up to your school trip, and know enough to spot the subtle difference between "*J'ai bien mangé, merci,*" ("I have had enough, thank you,") and "*Je suis un mangetout,*" (" I am a small, flat peapod, eaten whole,").

PROBLEM 2: When you can't afford to go on the school trip

● The scene

The rest of Baz's drama group has gone to see the new play by Bary Blokenev performed at The Watershed, the most fashionable theatre in the reclaimed former dockland area, about forty kilometres from St Herbert's. Baz wants to go very much indeed, but his mother says she cannot afford to pay for the trip. He tries phoning his father to ask for some help, but his father says that he has a bad financial headache and it isn't a good moment. How should Baz deal with the situation?

● **Bad reaction:** It is no use making your mother or father cry with guilt, because they would most likely pay for you to go if only they could, and are feeling bad enough about it already.

● **Equally bad reaction:** It is also a bad idea to rubbish the trip most of your friends are going on in a vain attempt to make yourself feel better about not going on it. "Gary WHO? Blokenev? Never heard of him. Apparently his stuff is rubbish. No one in their right mind would want to sit through three hours of THAT." You will only make yourself feel worse by adopting this attitude, because you'll just make yourself unpopular, and the people going on the trip won't want to listen to what you have to say (known as sour grapes).

● **Better idea:** Try to do something else special to cheer yourself up, such as taking the opportunity, while most of your friends are out of the way, to chat to the gorgeous boy/girl in year twelve who you fancy like mad (and so do your friends, so they usually get in the way, or embarrass you, or somehow make it difficult. But now they are forty kilometres away, so you can relax).

● **Another idea:** You could have a moan to others who cannot go, and maybe do something with them so you also have something to talk about.

● **A final thought:** It really is a NYCD situation (Nothing You Can Do About It). The best thing is to look forward to your friends getting back and telling them what you have been doing while they were away, as well as hearing how they got on. Let them tell you about the trip, as a few funny things are likely to have occurred which you may enjoy hearing about. Then you can tell them how you got chatting to the most beautiful boy/girl in the world, while they were away. But remember, life is not a competition about who has the best time. There are likely to be good moments and bad moments, no matter where you are or what you are doing (apparently the play was excellent, but weren't you lucky not to be on the coach coming home when Kevin Winterbotham was violently ill all over the floor).

The de-stress solutions to school trips:

1) Take a deep breath and count to ten. If you are in France, take a deep breath and count to *dix* (in German if you are in Germany, and so on).

2) Take something with you which reminds you of home. No, not your mother. Something small and special, to cuddle up to at night. No, not your hamster, either.

3) Take a Walkman and some of your favourite music to relax to at the end of a busy day.

4) Alternatively, close your eyes and listen to all the sounds around you, both familiar (birds singing/your mates arguing, and so on) and unfamiliar (people talking in another language, a different kind of bell ringing somewhere, a goat bleating – you don't have goats back at home). Letting your mind go blank, while listening to distant and nearby sounds, helps you to relax.

TAKE SOMETHING THAT REMINDS YOU OF HOME . . .

CHAPTER 7
Important Factors Affecting Your School Career

PROBLEM 1: Embarrassment factor (parents)

The Parents' Evening:

The scene

"Good evening, Mr Fogg. I just wanted to have a quiet word with you about my dear son Soumik. Come here, Soumik. Mr Fogg and I are a little worried."

"I'm not particularly worried about Soumik, Mrs Sen. At least, no more than anyone else is."

"Well, perhaps you should be! He has been having such difficulties with his homework. I am worried that he is overworking. Look at the great bags under his eyes. He is such a good-looking boy normally. And it is the French, particularly, which you teach that is most upsetting to him, because he is not understanding it."

"I teach geography, Mrs Sen."

"Oh. I'm so sorry."

"Don't be sorry. I quite enjoy it! Ha ha!"

At this, Mr and Mrs Sen both laugh over-loudly and immoderately in order to hide their embarrassment, succeeding only in causing further embarrassment, since

THE PARENTS' EVENING

everyone in the hall turns to look at them, including most of Soumik's friends.

Strategies for taking the stress out of the parents" evening:

1) Earlier in the day, hide the dreadful emerald-green coat with a fake-fur collar which you know that your mother was planning to wear this evening. You run the risk that she will delve deep into her wardrobe and produce something even worse, but you can attempt to steer her in the direction of something quiet and unremarkable. If you persuade your parents to wear brown, there is a chance that they might blend in with the floorboards and panelling in the school hall, so that fewer of your friends will actually notice them.

2) Develop a migraine/stomach ache/acute knee injury, so that you can stay at home and watch TV instead of accompanying your parents. But you can rest assured that they will blame your headache or any other kind of ache on the school and tell your year head that they are worried you are being put under too much pressure. "She needs sensitive handling, you know," they tell Mr Goodwood, whose arm is in plaster after you accidentally shut it in a door the other day.

3) Confess to your parents before they leave that the six pages of writing they saw you carefully working at in your room was not actually an essay on *Macbeth*. You were, in fact, copying out the school rules six times as punishment for eating a packet of Well Wicked flavour Crunchisnax in the library. (You were overheard by your year head, who was several rooms away at the time. Crunchisnax are LOUD, and you are not supposed to eat anywhere but in the canteen, except on wet days.) If you confess to your crimes before your parents go to the parents' evening, at least you won't have to wait uncomfortably for their return, wondering how much they have found out. Teachers seem determined to give away all the secrets which you had hoped were between you and the school, and your parents are equally keen to warble on at length about your little problems and funny little ways, and why they are not happy with the amount of homework you are being given (it is either too much or too little).

PROBLEM 2: Nuisance factor (siblings)

The scene

"Hey! Stevo! Spidershanks! Fathead! I need some money for lunch. I know Mum gave you some. Gimme! Gimme! Gimme five! Five pounds! HA HA! YEEE-HAH!"

This speech by James Cash, Steve's younger brother, demonstrates how easy it can be to suffer from sibling stress at school.

1) They shout at you and interrupt when you are just about to talk to the person you have, for a long time, admired from a distance.

2) They call you by an embarrassing pet name, previously known only to your family, or by a nickname which they know you can't stand.

3) They call you rude names.

4) They ask for money and never pay you back.

5) They leap about and grimace like apes.

6) They make silly noises.

REMEMBER THAT YOUNGER SIBLINGS PROBABLY LOOK UP TO YOU (EXCEPT WHEN THEY ARE DROPPING DREADFUL STUFF ON YOUR HEAD OUT OF THE CHEMISTRY LAB)

7) They reveal all your most embarrassing secrets.

How to steer clear of sibling stress at school:

1) Ignore them if they are in full pest mode. If they find they cannot easily wind you up, they will lose interest and leave you alone.

2) Bribe them before you even get to school and tell them they can have first go on your new computer game if they will kindly refrain from telling everyone that your pet name at home is Wibble.

3) Make sure that your parent has provided your sibling with everything they need, including money, so that you don't have to. Inevitably, of course, your sibling will lose their money/their schoolbag/their socks/their way through the building, and you will be called upon to come to their rescue. But doesn't it make you feel good to help them out?

Finally, there is Factor X:
(Watch out, watch out! There's a Big Head about!)

So what's going on inside your head? No one knows, but answer the following questions to find out a little more about heads in general:

1) Who is the real head of the school?

a) The headteacher.
b) The bursar or finance director.
c) The caretaker.
d) The dinner ladies.

Answer: All of the above, especially the bursar and the dinner ladies.

2) Mr Trusscott, the head of St Herbert's, is due to take early retirement. What changes have taken place at school during his time as headteacher?
a) He has aged about twenty years and developed a nervous twitch.

NO. 1 ENERGY-SAVING IDEA

b) Standards have risen in all areas.

c) CCTV (closed-circuit television) surveillance has been introduced to detect the activities of vandals and other wrongdoers.

d) The coveted Souper-duper Certificate of Extreme Excellence has been awarded to St Herbert's school canteen by the Healthy Schools Award Board.
e) St Herbert's has received the Green Award for energy-saving ideas.
f) Mr Trusscott is responsible for the introduction of clear perspex bike sheds and his own personal headicopter, so that he gets a good aerial perspective of the school. (The noise of the engine as he circles overhead tends to drown out the voice of any teacher addressing their class at the time.)

Answer: All of the above. It is a sad fact that the activities of a small number of wrongdoers can affect the whole school and give it a bad name (as if the name of St Herbert's is not bad enough). Mr Trusscott is determined that the introduction of CCTV and clear perspex bike sheds will put an end to this sort of thing. Not everyone is happy at the thought that Big Brother or Big Head will be watching them.

Spare a thought for the head (and other teachers): It must be a difficult job being head of a busy school, enough to give anyone a headache. Try not to add to their problems by behaving like a complete headcase. Why not help them to preserve their head cred?

In other words:

Don't do your head in!

The final de-stress solution:

1) Keep a cool head (if you have a cool head at your school, you are lucky!).

2) Head up, shoulders back, and keep your head down. Confused? Don't worry, so is everyone else.

MR TRUSSCOTT FLIES AWAY INTO THE SUNSET IN HIS HEADICOPTER

3) Don't forget to put your best foot forward (the one in the trainer which doesn't have a hole in the toe).

4) Get a good night's sleep. Head for bed and lay your weary head down on the pillow.

5) Realise that your schooldays won't last for ever (try not to cheer too loudly or you will disturb the whole household or, at least, the person sitting next to you). Seize every opportunity that school has to offer (including every opportunity to get out of it on a day trip and so on), and make a sincere and determined effort to enjoy yourself. In other words:

DO YOUR BEST!

Also available from Piccadilly Press by Kathryn Lamb:

HELP! MY FAMILY IS DRIVING ME CRAZY!
A Survival Guide For Teenagers

Families . . . At best, they curb your lifestyle. At worst, they drive you completely crazy.

Find out the tricks that Angelica Toogood, Basil Broke, Amy Average, Steve Cash and Soumik Sen use to deal with *their* ghastly families. You'll emerge happy and healthy, with your street cred intact!

Kathryn Lamb provides some invaluable tips on how to manage your family:

Parents respond well to flattery . . .
Bribery works wonders for siblings . . .
Prepare for potential problems, eg. warn parents that James is 'quite artistic' (has long hair, ten earrings and a tattoo) . . .
Learn the secret of really good answers - ones such as 'homework' and 'I want to be an accountant' work much better than 'nothing' or 'dunno'!

Always remember: **A happy parent is a kind and generous parent, a parent who likes to say "Yes!"**

"A little gem that we can all relate to. Filled with hilarious ways to get round your dreadful parents, keep them a happy and live a sane life yourself! Order us a job lot now!" - Mizz

Also available from Piccadilly Press by Kathryn Lamb:

HELP! MY SOCIAL LIFE IS A MESS!
A Survival Guide For Teenagers

Is your social life non-existent? Ruined by friends you don't like? Interrupted by school and homework? Or just in need of a bit of recuperation?

See how Basil Broke, Soumik Sen, Amy Average, Angelica Toogood and Steve Cash improve *their* lousy social lives in this essential guide.

But remember . . . Your idea of what your social life should be (the party scene, fantastic boy/girlfriend, fun! fun! fun!, forget to sleep, don't worry Mum/Dad, I'll be back by 4a.m.) may differ in some respects from your parents' idea.

So don't worry a parent. A worried parent is a problem parent, a parent who likes to say "No!"